Multisensory Teaching of Basic Language Skills
Activity Book
Fourth Edition

Multisensory Teaching of Basic Language Skills Activity Book

Fourth Edition

by

Suzanne Carreker, Ph.D., CALT-QI
Principal Educational Lead, Lexia Learning Systems
Concord, Massachusetts

and

Judith R. Birsh, Ed.D., CALT-QI
Independent Literacy Consultant
New York, New York

·P·A·U·L·H·
BROOKES
PUBLISHING CO.®

Baltimore • London • Sydney

Paul H. Brookes Publishing Co.
Post Office Box 10624
Baltimore, Maryland 21285-0624
USA

www.brookespublishing.com

Typeset by Progressive Publishing Services, York, Pennsylvania.
Manufactured in the United States of America by
Sheridan Books, Inc. Chelsea, Michigan.

Cover photo and Figures 95.1 and 97.1 photos © iStockphoto.com.

The individuals described in this book are composites or real people whose situations are masked and are based on the authors' experiences. In all instances, names and identifying details have been changed to protect confidentiality.

A companion textbook, *Multisensory Teaching of Basic Language Skills, Fourth Edition* (ISBN-13: 978-1-68125-226-1), edited by Judith R. Birsh and Suzanne Carreker, is also available from Paul H. Brookes Publishing Co. (1-800-638-3775; 1-410-337-9580). For more information on the Multisensory Teaching of Basic Language Skills materials, go to www.brookespublishing.com.

Library of Congress Cataloging-in-Publication Data

Names: Carreker, Suzanne, author. | Birsh, Judith R., author.
Title: Multisensory teaching of basic language skills activity book / by Suzanne Carreker, Ph.D., and Judith R. Birsh, Ed.D.
Description: Fourth edition. | Baltimore: Paul H. Brookes Publishing Co., [2019] | Includes bibliographical references and index.
Identifiers: LCCN 2018024606 | ISBN 9781681253084 (pbk.)
Subjects: LCSH: Dyslexic children–Education–United States. | Dyslexics–Education–United States. | Language art–United States.
Classification: LCC LC4708.85 .C37 2019 | DDC 372.6–dc23
LC record available at https://lccn.loc.gov/2018024606

British Library Cataloguing in Publication data are available from the British Library.

2022   2021   2020

10   9   8   7   6   5   4   3   2

Contents

About the Online Companion Materials

Purchasers of this book may download, print, and/or photocopy the materials provided in the Online Companion Materials (OCM) for educational use. The materials found in Appendices A through O are included with the print book and are also available at www.brookespublishing.com/carreker/materials for both print and e-book buyers.

About the Authors

Suzanne Carreker, Ph.D., Certified Academic Language Therapist (CALT), Qualified Instructor (QI), Principal Educational Lead, Lexia Learning Systems, Concord, Massachusetts

Dr. Carreker is developing content for blended-learning reading programs at Lexia Learning Systems. Her passion for teaching reading began with an impromptu opportunity to attend a lecture given by dyslexia pioneer Margaret Byrd Rawson. She taught at Briarwood School in Houston, Texas, and directed teacher preparation programs at Neuhaus Education Center in Houston for 28 years. During her second year of teaching, Dr. Carreker attended a 1-hour workshop presented by the three Neuhaus founders that led to her preparation as a CALT and QI at the center. Dr. Carreker believes that teachers' deep knowledge about reading and skill in teaching reading should not be the result of serendipity. To that end, Dr. Carreker served on the committee for the development of The International Dyslexia Association's (IDA) *Knowledge and Practice Standards for Teachers of Reading* and led the development of the Certification Exam for Effective Teaching of Reading—both guideposts for pre-service and in-service teacher preparation programs. She was the 2009 HBIDA Nancy LaFevers Community Service Award recipient for her contributions to students with dyslexia and related learning differences in the Houston area. In 2018, she received the Margaret Byrd Rawson Lifetime Achievement Award from the IDA.

Judith R. Birsh, Ed.D., Certified Academic Language Therapist (CALT), Qualified Instructor (QI), Independent Literacy Consultant, 333 West 86th Street, New York, New York

Dr. Birsh was the editor of the first three editions of *Multisensory Teaching of Basic Language Skills*. Her enduring belief that well-prepared, informed teachers are the major influence on effective instruction in the field of reading and dyslexia had its beginning in 1960, when she met her first student who, although 18 years old, read poorly. The quest to find answers to this puzzle led her to a master's degree in remedial reading and a doctorate in reading and language at Teachers College, Columbia University. After training with Aylett R. Cox in Dallas, Texas, she became a Certified Academic Language Therapist and Qualified Instructor, founding and directing the multisensory teaching of basic language skills courses at Teachers College in the Department of Curriculum and Teaching, Program in Learning Disabilities. Since her retirement in 2000, Dr. Birsh has maintained her commitment to teacher preparation as an independent literacy consultant, by giving professional development workshops, consulting with private and public schools, writing articles, and working with students with dyslexia. In 2008, she received the Luke Waites Academic Language Therapy Association Award of Service and the Margaret Byrd Rawson Lifetime Achievement Award from The International Dyslexia Association.

Introduction

The purpose of the fourth edition of the *Multisensory Teaching of Basic Language Skills Activity Book* is to help reinforce the information gained during teacher preparation from texts, classroom lectures, and practicums. These activities provide teachers with opportunities to reflect on and assimilate newly acquired linguistic concepts, along with a check of their knowledge and practice skills for teaching Structured Literacy that are aligned with *Knowledge and Practice Standards for Teachers of Reading* (International Dyslexia Association [IDA], 2018). In addition, the activities can act as a platform from which to plan lessons with these concepts for their students.

Teacher knowledge is essential to student success (Brady & Moats, 1997; IDA, 2018; Piasta, Connor, Fishman, & Morrison, 2009). Teachers must understand the theoretical underpinnings of literacy acquisition. They must know effective methods for teaching literacy skills and ways to differentiate their instruction to meet the needs of all students. Teachers themselves must possess underlying linguistic skills and insights about different language structures so that they can successfully instruct their students. The textbook *Multisensory Teaching of Basic Language Skills, Fourth Edition* (Birsh & Carreker, 2018), provides teachers with current research findings and specific multisensory methods of instruction in all areas of literacy. This activity book is a supplement to that textbook and contains activities that reinforce and extend the information presented in it. The activities are designed to target and refine necessary linguistic skills and insights about language structures that teachers need to know to ensure that their students know them, too. In addition, the activities are also coordinated with Chapters 3–8 of the textbook *Becoming a Professional Reading Teacher* (Aaron, Joshi, & Quatroche, 2008).

The section "Activities Arranged by Structured Literacy Components" on the following pages coordinates the activities in the workbook with the chapters in the Birsh and Carreker (2018) textbook. Readers can progress through the chapters in that textbook and, as they finish each chapter, complete the activities that relate to that chapter, or readers can complete the exercises in this activity book in order and then read and refer to the related chapters in the textbook. For each activity, an icon appearing at the top right corner indicates the chapter(s) from the textbook that would be particularly helpful for users to refer to while completing the activity. Some activities also include referrals to a teacher web site that offer readers demonstrations of teachers engaged in teaching those concepts.

All of the activities are designed to enhance teachers' knowledge base. The reason some activities, purposefully, have more than one chapter reference is that knowledge about Structured Literacy overlaps from content area to content area, reinforcing the interrelatedness of the information. Some activities can be adapted for use with students. For example, interspersed among the activities are 19 Try This exercises designed specifically for use with students in the classroom or small-group settings. Furthermore, Appendixes A–O contain many resources teachers can use to enhance their own understanding of linguistic concepts and their presentation to their students. There are reproducible games, charts, graphic organizers, word lists, comprehension passages, and templates for lesson plans. The appendices included with the print book are also available as Online Companion Materials (OCM) on the companion web site for this book at www.brookespublishing.com/carreker/materials for both print and e-book buyers. Finally, there is an Answer Key for all of the activities so that teachers can check their understanding while they are learning new skills.

A guide to activities coordinated with the Aaron et al. (2008) textbook can be found at the end of the Answer Key.

NOTE TO MULTISENSORY STRUCTURED LANGUAGE EDUCATORS

Some of the activities in the workbook share the same title. For example, Activities 17 and 18 are both titled *Phoneme Checklist*. In a training setting, participants complete the first activity for practice. The second activity with the same title could be completed as an assessment.

REFERENCES

Aaron, P.G., Joshi, R.M., & Quatroche, D. (2008). *Becoming a professional reading teacher*. Baltimore, MD: Paul H. Brookes Publishing Co.

Birsh, J.R., & Carreker, S. (Eds.). (2018). *Multisensory teaching of basic language skills* (4th ed.). Baltimore, MD: Paul H. Brookes Publishing Co.

Brady, S., & Moats, L.C. (1997). *Informed instruction for reading success: Foundations for teacher preparation* (A position paper of The International Dyslexia Association). Baltimore, MD: The International Dyslexia Association.

International Dyslexia Association, The. (2018, March). *Knowledge and practice standards for teachers of reading*. Retrieved from https://dyslexiaida.org/knowledge-and-practices/

Piasta, S.B., Connor, C.M., Fishman, B.J., & Morrison, F.J. (2009). Teachers' knowledge of literary concepts, classroom practices, and student reading growth. *Scientific Studies of Reading, 13*(3), 224–248.

Activities Arranged by Structured Literacy Components

Emergent Literacy (Chapter 4)

Activities: 6, 7

English Language Learners (Chapter 19)

Activity: 101

Executive Function (Chapter 8)

Activities: 21, 22, 23, 24

Fluency (Chapter 12)

Activities: 70, 71, 72

Try This I

Handwriting (Chapter 11)

Activities: 65, 66, 67, 68, 69

History and Structure of Written English (Chapter 14)

Activities 74, 75, 76, 77, 78, 79

Try This J

Try This K

Lesson Planning (Chapter 18)

Activities: 64, 69, 99, 100

Mathematics (Chapter 13)

Activity 73

Morphology (Chapters 14 and 15)

Activities: 74, 75, 76, 77, 78, 79, 80

Try This L

Multisensory Teaching (Chapter 2)

Activities: 1, 5, 9, 10, 16, 25, 26, 28, 33, 34, 38, 39, 40, 41, 49, 52, 53, 54, 55, 60, 66, 81, 82, 83, 84, 88

Try This H

(*Note:* Most of the activities in this book contain multisensory/multimodal elements to practice.)

Oral Language (Chapter 3)

Activity: 4

Phonological Awareness and Phonemes (Chapter 6)

Activities: 5, 8, 9, 10, 11, 12, 13, 14, 15, 16, 17, 18, 19, 52, 53, 54, 55

Spelling (Chapter 10)

Activities: 56, 57, 58, 59, 60, 61, 62, 63, 64

Try This H

Vocabulary (Chapter 15)

Activities: 74, 75, 76, 77, 78, 79, 80, 81, 82, 83, 84, 85, 86, 87, 88, 89

Try This L

Try This M

Try This N

Try This O

Try This P

Working With Older Students and Adults (Chapters 20 and 21)

Activities: 2, 12, 14, 25 to 64, 70, 71, 72, 77, 78, 79, 87, 88, 89, 90, 91, 102, 103

Try This H

Try This J

Terms for Research and Structured Literacy

Match each term with the correct definition. Use Chapters 1 and 2 in *Multisensory Teaching of Basic Language Skills, Fourth Edition* (Birsh & Carreker, 2018) for reference.

1. _____ Structured Literacy

2. _____ qualitative research

3. _____ quantitative research

4. _____ experimental research

5. _____ quasi-experimental research

6. _____ metacognition

7. _____ Broca's area

8. _____ parieto-temporal

9. _____ occipito-temporal

10. _____ auditory

11. _____ visual

12. _____ modality

13. _____ kinesthetic

14. _____ multisensory

15. _____ tactile

16. _____ word blindness

17. _____ explicit instruction

18. _____ dyslexia

a. Area of the brain for articulation

b. Related to muscle movement and memory

c. Early term for dyslexia

d. Area of the brain for word analysis

e. A specific sensory pathway

f. Related to touch

g. Area of the brain for word form

h. Related to seeing

i. Pertaining to the simultaneous use of multiple senses

j. Clear, precise, and specific instruction

k. Research in which the subjects are randomly assigned to experimental and control groups

l. Deliberate rearrangement of information while thinking

m. Research conducted without randomized assignment of subjects to experimental and control groups

n. Related to hearing

o. A specific language-based disorder characterized by difficulty with single-word reading

p. Research in which results are based on a large sample that is representative of the population

q. Research that collects data through various kinds of observations

r. A comprehensive, research-based framework for instruction focused on the structure of language to teach reading

Appendix A of this activity book summarizes the major findings of recent research and may be photocopied for informational purposes and distributed to educators, administrators, and parents.

The Brain

Multiple sites in the brain are activated when a student reads. The different sites perform specific functions during reading and rely on connections with other sites. Research has shown that there are neural abnormalities in the language areas of the left hemisphere in a student with a language-based reading disability (Farrell & Cushen-White, 2018; Rumsey, 1996).

Use Figure 2.1 to label the various parts of the brain and their function in terms of reading. Use Chapters 1 and 2 of Birsh and Carreker (2018) for reference.

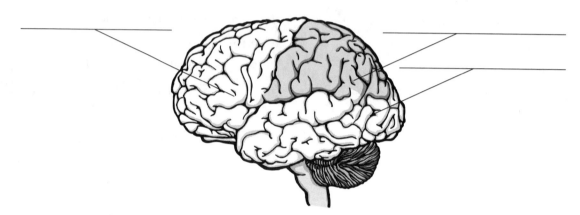

Figure 2.1. The brain's four cortical lobes. (From Kaufman, C. [2011]. *Executive function in the classroom: Practical strategies for improving performance and enhancing skills for all students* [p. 27]. Baltimore, MD: Paul H. Brookes Publishing Co.; reprinted by permission.)

Structured Literacy Terms

Match each term with the correct definition. Use Chapters 6 and 9 in Birsh and Carreker (2018).

1. _____ phonetics
2. _____ phonology
3. _____ allophone
4. _____ phonological awareness
5. _____ phonics
6. _____ phoneme
7. _____ phonemic awareness
8. _____ alphabetic principle
9. _____ grapheme
10. _____ consonant
11. _____ vowel
12. _____ RAN
13. _____ double deficit
14. _____ guided discovery teaching

a. Smallest unit of sound in a syllable

b. Instruction that connects sounds and letters

c. The rules that determine how sounds are used in spoken language

d. Study of the characteristics of speech sounds

e. The understanding that spoken sounds are represented in print by letters

f. Awareness of the overall sound structure of words

g. A variation of a speech sound

h. Awareness of speech sounds or phonemes in spoken words

i. Rapid automatized naming

j. A class of speech sounds with air flow that is constricted or obstructed

k. A method of leading students to new learning through questioning

l. A letter or letter cluster that represents a single speech sound

m. A class of open speech sounds produced by the passage of air through an open vocal tract

n. Deficit in phonological awareness and rapid naming

Terms for Oral Language

Match each term with the correct definition. Use Chapter 3 in Birsh and Carreker (2018) for reference.

1. _____ metalinguistic

2. _____ aspiration

3. _____ suprasegmentals

4. _____ pragmatics

5. _____ affixes

6. _____ dyspraxia

7. _____ phonology, morphology, syntax

8. _____ dysarthria

9. _____ schwa

10. _____ semantics

a. Speech problems caused by sensorimotor disruption

b. The melody of speech—stress, pitch, loudness, and so forth

c. The sound /ə/

d. Content of language

e. Puff of air

f. Awareness of language as an entity

g. Use of language

h. Prefixes and suffixes

i. Speech problems caused by musculature weaknesses

j. Domains of language

Phonemes: Vowels

Vowel sounds are created with positions of the jaw, tongue, and lips (Moats, 1995, 2010; Soifer, 2018). The jaw opens to varying degrees. The tongue may be front or back and high or low. The lips may be rounded or not rounded. The awareness of the speech features helps with the pronunciation and identification of speech sounds. Fill in the missing vowels in Figure 5.1, the Vowel Chart. Notice the positions of your jaw, tongue, and lips as you say each vowel sound. Use Chapter 3 in Birsh and Carreker (2018) for reference.

Front, smiley ☐
see
these
me
eat
key
happy
chief
either

☐
Sit
gym

☐
make
rain
play
baby
eight
vein
great
they

☐
pet
head

☐
cat

☐
about
lesson
elect
definition
circus

☐
time
pie
right
rifle
by
buy
heist

☐
fox
father
palm

☐
cup
cover
flood
tough

☐
saw
pause
call
water
daughter
thought

☐
vote
doe
boat
snow
open
though

☐
took
put
could

☐
moo
tube
blue
chew
ruby
suit
soup

☐
music
mute Back, rounded
few
Europe

☐☐
boy, oil
cow, out, bough

Low, open

☐
sir
her, letter
fur

☐
car

☐
organ

Figure 5.1. Vowel Chart. (From Moats, LC. [2010]. *Speech to print: Language essentials for teachers* [2nd ed., p. 96]. Baltimore, MD: Paul H. Brookes Publishing Co.; adapted by permission.)

What Children Know
and What They Can Explore

Think about two subjects. Brainstorm things preschool children might know about the subject and what they might like to explore about the subject. An example is provided for you.

Subject	What children know	What children can explore
Squirrels	Squirrels are grey.	Where do squirrels live?
	They hop.	Can we find baby squirrels?
	They're good jumpers.	When they jump from tree to tree do they ever fall?
	They eat acorns.	Why are their tails so big?
Birds	Birds have feathers.	Do all birds have feathers?
	They make different sounds.	What birds live near our playground?
	They have two wings.	Can all birds fly?
	Birds fly in the air.	Where are the birds going that fly in big groups?

Subject	What children know	What children can explore

Open-Ended Questions

Closed-ended questions generally can be answered in a word or two: *What is your favorite fruit? What did you build?* Open-ended questions encourage young learners to use more language as well as higher level thinking skills: *Why is an apple your favorite fruit? How did you build your tower?*

Write examples of closed-ended questions. Then, change the closed-ended questions into open-ended questions that will require more than a word or two to answer and will encourage higher level thinking skills.

Closed-ended question	Open-ended question

Letter Shapes and Names

Calling attention to how letters look aids students in their ability to instantly recognize letters. Printed letters are composed of all straight lines, all curved lines, or a combination of straight and curved lines. Write each uppercase, or capital, letter of the alphabet in the column that best describes the letter. Then, do the same with the lowercase printed letters. Then, complete Try This A.

All straight lines	All curved lines	Straight and curved lines
A	C	B

TRY THIS

A   Instant Letter Recognition

1. Make a photocopy of the Instant Letter-Recognition Chart in Appendix B.
2. Fill the chart with six letters that repeat in a different order in each row.
3. Prepare the chart as an overhead transparency or on an interactive whiteboard.
4. Touch and name the letters in the first row.
5. Touch the letters in the first row as students name them.
6. Start again at the top. Touch the letters as quickly possible, working across each row and down the chart, row by row.
7. Time the students for 1 minute.
8. The initial goal is for students to read the chart two times in 1 minute. The goal for students in Grades 3 and higher is to read the chart four times in 1 minute.

Chapter 6

Phonemic Awareness Activities

Phonological awareness is a broad term that describes the sound structure of language. Phonological awareness skills develop hierarchically from rhyming to syllable counting to detecting and manipulating phonemes (Paulson, 2018). Activities that specifically deal with phonemes in words are referred to as *phonemic awareness activities*. Review the 12 phonemic awareness activities below. Then, sort them by type. Place the number of the activity in the correct column.

1. What word is /m/…/ă/…/t/?
2. Change the /l/ in *lip* to /s/.
3. What sounds are in *mat*?
4. What word does not belong: *make, miss, tip*?
5. What is *stop* without /s/?
6. What is the medial sound of *cat*?
7. How many sounds are in *cheek*?
8. What is the first sound in *lamp*?
9. Add /s/ to the beginning of *lip*.
10. Which word has three sounds: *ship* or *last*?
11. What is the final sound in *pig*?
12. What word is /c/…/l/…/ŏ/…/k/?

Isolation/identification	Blending	Segmentation	Deletion/addition

How Many Phonemes?

A phoneme is the smallest unit of sound that distinguishes one word from another. A beginning reader's ability to segment a word into its constituent phonemes is one of the best predictors of reading success. How many phonemes are represented in each word?

1. mat   _____
2. cash   _____
3. ship   _____
4. match   _____
5. stop   _____
6. knife   _____
7. scratch   _____
8. truck   _____
9. love   _____
10. spell   _____

11. stand   _____
12. child   _____
13. month   _____
14. think   _____
15. peach   _____
16. queen   _____
17. train   _____
18. climb   _____
19. strike   _____
20. blank   _____

How Many Phonemes?

How many phonemes are represented in each word?

1. show _____
2. splint _____
3. knee _____
4. badge _____
5. past _____
6. face _____
7. thrill _____
8. clock _____
9. give _____
10. shack _____

11. strand _____
12. teeth _____
13. church _____
14. shrink _____
15. enough _____
16. quit _____
17. fix _____
18. smile _____
19. night _____
20. flax _____

ACTIVITY 12

Same Phoneme?

The same phoneme can be represented with different graphemes. The same grapheme can represent more than one phoneme. There are variations of some phonemes that can be represented by the same grapheme. These variants are called *allophones* and are not separate phonemes. For example, the phoneme represented by initial *p* in the word *pop* is a slight variation of the phoneme represented by final *p*. The initial phoneme is aspirated as /pʰ/. The final phoneme is /p/.

Look at the underlined graphemes in each pair of words below. Do the underlined graphemes in each pair represent the same phoneme, do they represent different phonemes, or is one of the phonemes an allophone? If the underlined graphemes in a pair represent the same phoneme, write *yes*. If the underlined graphemes in a pair represent different phonemes, or if one of the phonemes is an allophone, write *no*.

		Same?				**Same?**
1.	s<u>ai</u>d	b<u>e</u>d	_____	11.	ar<u>ch</u>	e<u>ch</u>o	_____
2.	<u>s</u>pins	spin<u>s</u>	_____	12.	splin<u>t</u>	jump<u>ed</u>	_____
3.	ba<u>th</u>	sa<u>f</u>e	_____	13.	si<u>n</u>k	si<u>ng</u>	_____
4.	st<u>ea</u>k	v<u>ei</u>n	_____	14.	fi<u>r</u>st	fe<u>r</u>n	_____
5.	ni<u>gh</u>t	t<u>ie</u>	_____	15.	ten<u>s</u>e	fa<u>c</u>e	_____
6.	m<u>ar</u>ket	must<u>ar</u>d	_____	16.	fl<u>y</u>	penn<u>y</u>	_____
7.	<u>th</u>at	<u>v</u>ase	_____	17.	rh<u>y</u>thm	rh<u>y</u>me	_____
8.	p<u>ea</u>ch	pr<u>ie</u>st	_____	18.	<u>z</u>ipper	pan<u>s</u>y	_____
9.	pl<u>ai</u>d	bl<u>a</u>st	_____	19.	gra<u>f</u>t	gra<u>ph</u>	_____
10.	<u>o</u>rbit	act<u>o</u>r	_____	20.	land<u>ed</u>	seem<u>ed</u>	_____

Same Phoneme?

Look at the underlined graphemes in each pair of words. If the underlined graphemes represent the same phoneme, write *yes* beside each pair. If the underlined graphemes represent different phonemes or if one of the phonemes is an allophone, write *no* beside each pair.

	Same?				Same?
1.	v<u>ie</u>w	sh<u>oe</u>	_____	11.	<u>th</u>at	wi<u>th</u>	_____
2.	w<u>a</u>sh	m<u>a</u>sh	_____	12.	si<u>ng</u>le	fi<u>ng</u>er	_____
3.	<u>t</u>ent	ten<u>t</u>	_____	13.	<u>j</u>eep	<u>g</u>irl	_____
4.	bo<u>y</u>	b<u>oi</u>l	_____	14.	r<u>aw</u>	h<u>au</u>l	_____
5.	can<u>y</u>on	<u>y</u>ellow	_____	15.	<u>g</u>em	<u>j</u>et	_____
6.	doct<u>or</u>	sh<u>or</u>tage	_____	16.	w<u>a</u>ter	p<u>o</u>lish	_____
7.	<u>sh</u>ack	wa<u>sh</u>	_____	17.	hea<u>l</u>	hea<u>l</u>th	_____
8.	<u>i</u>sle	sp<u>y</u>	_____	18.	gr<u>ou</u>p	gr<u>ou</u>t	_____
9.	r<u>oo</u>m	fr<u>ui</u>t	_____	19.	tr<u>oo</u>p	s<u>ou</u>p	_____
10.	balle<u>t</u>	surv<u>ey</u>	_____	20.	ga<u>s</u>	hi<u>s</u>	_____

How Many Letters and How Many Phonemes?

The number of letters and the number of phonemes in a word may differ. Write the number of letters and the number of phonemes for each word.

		Letters	Phonemes				Letters	Phonemes
1.	broom	_____	_____		11.	mix	_____	_____
2.	knee	_____	_____		12.	show	_____	_____
3.	shrimp	_____	_____		13.	left	_____	_____
4.	splint	_____	_____		14.	child	_____	_____
5.	sprint	_____	_____		15.	space	_____	_____
6.	lead	_____	_____		16.	teach	_____	_____
7.	grasp	_____	_____		17.	both	_____	_____
8.	sound	_____	_____		18.	spend	_____	_____
9.	blame	_____	_____		19.	kind	_____	_____
10.	sing	_____	_____		20.	knowledge	_____	_____

How Many Letters and How Many Phonemes?

TEXTBOOK REFERENCE
Chapters 9, 10, and 20

Write the number of letters and the number of phonemes for each word.

		Letters	Phonemes				Letters	Phonemes
1.	judge	_____	_____		11.	most	_____	_____
2.	need	_____	_____		12.	shout	_____	_____
3.	peach	_____	_____		13.	shrill	_____	_____
4.	thrill	_____	_____		14.	less	_____	_____
5.	know	_____	_____		15.	close	_____	_____
6.	plan	_____	_____		16.	cloth	_____	_____
7.	clasp	_____	_____		17.	splice	_____	_____
8.	knife	_____	_____		18.	trend	_____	_____
9.	may	_____	_____		19.	jacket	_____	_____
10.	stray	_____	_____		20.	muskrat	_____	_____

Phonemes
Voiced and Unvoiced Consonants

Some sounds activate the vocal cords during production. These sounds are referred to as *voiced*. Some sounds do not activate the vocal cords during production. These sounds are referred to as *unvoiced*. Write the following consonant sounds in the appropriate column.

/b/   /ch/   /d/   /f/   /g/   /h/   /hw/   /j/   /k/   /l/   /m/   /n/   /ng/

/p/   /r/   /s/   /sh/   /t/   /th/   /<u>th</u>/   /v/   /w/   /y/   /z/   /zh/

Voiced	Unvoiced

Phoneme Checklist

This checklist incorporates characteristics of sounds in English. Understanding the characteristics can aid accurate spelling. For example, /m/ is blocked, voiced, and a continuant, and /p/ is partially blocked, unvoiced, and clipped.

/l/ as in *leaf*
- ❑ open
- ❑ voiced
- ❑ continuant
- ❑ partially blocked
- ❑ unvoiced
- ❑ clipped
- ❑ blocked

/d/ as in *dog*
- ❑ open
- ❑ voiced
- ❑ continuant
- ❑ partially blocked
- ❑ unvoiced
- ❑ clipped
- ❑ blocked

/g/ as in *goat*
- ❑ open
- ❑ voiced
- ❑ continuant
- ❑ partially blocked
- ❑ unvoiced
- ❑ clipped
- ❑ blocked

/b/ as in *bat*
- ❑ open
- ❑ voiced
- ❑ continuant
- ❑ partially blocked
- ❑ unvoiced
- ❑ clipped
- ❑ blocked

/th/ as in *thin*
- ❑ open
- ❑ voiced
- ❑ continuant
- ❑ partially blocked
- ❑ unvoiced
- ❑ clipped
- ❑ blocked

/ch/ as in *chin*
- ❑ open
- ❑ voiced
- ❑ continuant
- ❑ partially blocked
- ❑ unvoiced
- ❑ clipped
- ❑ blocked

/w/ as in *wagon*
- ❑ open
- ❑ voiced
- ❑ continuant
- ❑ partially blocked
- ❑ unvoiced
- ❑ clipped
- ❑ blocked

/h/ as in *house*
- ❑ open
- ❑ voiced
- ❑ partially blocked
- ❑ unvoiced
- ❑ blocked

/m/ as in *mitten*
- ❑ open
- ❑ voiced
- ❑ continuant
- ❑ partially blocked
- ❑ unvoiced
- ❑ clipped
- ❑ blocked

/j/ as in *jump*
- ❑ open
- ❑ voiced
- ❑ continuant
- ❑ partially blocked
- ❑ unvoiced
- ❑ clipped
- ❑ blocked

/zh/ as in *erosion*
- ❑ open
- ❑ voiced
- ❑ continuant
- ❑ partially blocked
- ❑ unvoiced
- ❑ clipped
- ❑ blocked

/s/ as in *sock*
- ❑ open
- ❑ voiced
- ❑ continuant
- ❑ partially blocked
- ❑ unvoiced
- ❑ clipped
- ❑ blocked

Phoneme Checklist

Check the appropriate descriptions for each phoneme listed below.

/y/ as in *yellow*
- ❏ open
- ❏ voiced
- ❏ continuant
- ❏ partially blocked
- ❏ unvoiced
- ❏ clipped
- ❏ blocked

/z/ as in *zipper*
- ❏ open
- ❏ voiced
- ❏ continuant
- ❏ partially blocked
- ❏ unvoiced
- ❏ clipped
- ❏ blocked

/n/ as in *nest*
- ❏ open
- ❏ voiced
- ❏ continuant
- ❏ partially blocked
- ❏ unvoiced
- ❏ clipped
- ❏ blocked

/ng/ as in *sink*
- ❏ open
- ❏ voiced
- ❏ continuant
- ❏ partially blocked
- ❏ unvoiced
- ❏ clipped
- ❏ blocked

/k/ as in *kite*
- ❏ open
- ❏ voiced
- ❏ continuant
- ❏ partially blocked
- ❏ unvoiced
- ❏ clipped
- ❏ blocked

/p/ as in *pig*
- ❏ open
- ❏ voiced
- ❏ continuant
- ❏ partially blocked
- ❏ unvoiced
- ❏ clipped
- ❏ blocked

/sh/ as in *ship*
- ❏ open
- ❏ voiced
- ❏ continuant
- ❏ partially blocked
- ❏ unvoiced
- ❏ clipped
- ❏ blocked

/t/ as in *table*
- ❏ open
- ❏ voiced
- ❏ continuant
- ❏ partially blocked
- ❏ unvoiced
- ❏ clipped
- ❏ blocked

/f/ as in *fish*
- ❏ open
- ❏ voiced
- ❏ continuant
- ❏ partially blocked
- ❏ unvoiced
- ❏ clipped
- ❏ blocked

/th/ as in *mother*
- ❏ open
- ❏ voiced
- ❏ continuant
- ❏ partially blocked
- ❏ unvoiced
- ❏ clipped
- ❏ blocked

/v/ as in *valentine*
- ❏ open
- ❏ voiced
- ❏ continuant
- ❏ partially blocked
- ❏ unvoiced
- ❏ clipped
- ❏ blocked

/r/ as in *rabbit*
- ❏ open
- ❏ voiced
- ❏ continuant
- ❏ partially blocked
- ❏ unvoiced
- ❏ clipped
- ❏ blocked

Classification of Phonemes

Match the terms with the appropriate definition.

1. _____ nasal
2. _____ stop
3. _____ fricative
4. _____ affricate
5. _____ glide
6. _____ liquid

a. A consonant sound that consists of a slowly released stop followed by a fricative

b. A sound produced by forcing air through the nose

c. A sound produced by forcing air through a narrow opening between the teeth and lips to make a hissing sound

d. A sound produced when the lips and/or tongue are passing from the position for one sound to that of another

e. A sound in which the outgoing air flow is completely stopped

f. A flowing and vowel-like sound

Match the sounds with their classification.

7. _____ /t/, /k/
8. _____ /n/, /m/
9. _____ /f/, /z/
10. _____ /ch/, /j/
11. _____ /w/, /y/
12. _____ /l/, /r/

g. nasals
h. affricates
i. stops
j. fricatives
k. liquids
l. glides

Terms for Assessment

Match each term with the correct definition. Use Chapter 7 in Birsh and Carreker (2018) for reference.

1. _____ norm-referenced test
2. _____ criterion-referenced test
3. _____ curriculum-referenced test
4. _____ screening
5. _____ progress monitoring
6. _____ standard scores
7. _____ RAN
8. _____ formal assessment
9. _____ informal assessment
10. _____ validity
11. _____ formative data
12. _____ summative data
13. _____ DIBELS
14. _____ reliability
15. _____ PALS

a. Dynamic Indicators of Basic Literacy Skills (Good & Kiminski, 2002)

b. Periodic assessment that measures progress in response to specific instruction

c. The consistencies of test results

d. Brief assessment that identifies students who may need additional or alternate forms of instruction

e. Assessment that measures knowledge attained and knowledge yet to be acquired in a domain

f. The meaning that can be assigned to a test result; the test actually measures what it claims to measure

g. Standardized assessment that must be administered and scored according to prescribed procedures

h. Phonological Awareness Literacy Screening (Invernizzi, Meier, & Juel, 2002)

i. Data that provide information about knowledge to be applied to long-term, comprehensive goals

j. Data that provide information about knowledge to be applied to short-term goals

k. Assessment that measures knowledge that has been taught

l. Assessment that classifies a student in terms of achievement or improvement of grade-level performance

m. Address a student's change in performance relative to the mean rate of change for other students of his or her age or grade

n. Assessment that measures performance in relation to a norm cohort or group

o. Assessments that are not standardized

Executive Function

Language

TEXTBOOK REFERENCE

Chapter 8

Monica Gordon-Pershey

Language skills are fundamental to learning in an organized fashion. Language helps learners plan what to do, govern what they do, and review what they have done. Mariam is a 12-year-old girl who was diagnosed with a specific language impairment when she was 4 years old and with a coexisting diagnosis of specific learning disability when she was 7 years old. She has been included in general education with special education supports and speech-language pathology services throughout her schooling. Her vocabulary and concept development are adequate for her grade level, but her language deficits make it difficult for her to develop the organizational skills that are required in middle school. As such, she has difficulty completing assignments and keeping up with school demands. For example, she confuses items on her class schedule, struggles to know how to independently start her classwork or homework assignments, and has trouble organizing her ideas to complete her written work, such as writing answers to test questions and composing her learning journal entries. Mariam and her teachers tend to describe her as "lost." Her teachers try to help her employ language as a tool to become better organized and to use other multisensory organizational strategies.

Explain how Mariam's challenges relate to both executive functioning and language. Which of the teaching and learning strategies might improve Mariam's organizational skills and academic performance?

Executive Function
Working Memory

Monica Gordon-Pershey

Working memory involves integrating one's recollections of past learning experiences with present contexts. In middle school and high school academic contexts, much of students' past learning derives from texts they have read. Consider the links between reading comprehension and working memory: Accurate reading comprehension allows for storing useful information; subsequent recall of information allows for its use to comprehend new texts. Working memory is operative to make reading comprehension possible; it regulates how readers recall and apply past learnings and store incoming new information.

Consider the case of Maya, a 13-year-old student who has difficulty with reading comprehension related to a weakness in recalling and applying prior readings to new learnings. Maya appears to make very few connections across the texts she reads. Her teachers are exploring how to use multisensory strategies to help her activate prior knowledge and build a body of information on a topic. How can Maya's teachers help her learn strategies so she can independently demonstrate more efficient and accurate recall of past learnings? Use Figure 8.3 in Birsh and Carreker (2018), along with the information provided throughout Chapter 8, to identify and describe the locus of Maya's challenges and as the basis for brainstorming learning strategies for her to use.

Executive Function

Making Connections

Monica Gordon-Pershey

Abraham is an 11-year-old boy who has difficulty considering alternative forms of information. He is somewhat rigid and inflexible in his thinking. For example, he has difficulty seeing multiplication and division as inverse processes. He can multiply and divide, but he finds it difficult to use the processes reciprocally or in a complementary fashion. Abraham's teachers use verbalization as a strategy to help him translate concepts into words and find that this provides a window into observing his reasoning. They conclude that Abraham has trouble organizing concepts; the teachers call this a weakness in "thinking for connections."

Abraham's teachers observe that in emotional and social circumstances, Abraham may have difficulty understanding how competing conditions might exist. The teachers note that Abraham stated that he did not understand why some students were both happy and sad at the end of the school year; it could not be both, in his reasoning. His teachers employ strategies to promote critical thinking, inferential thinking, perspective taking, generating alternatives, and metacognitive questioning, and they help him become aware of how flexibility in reasoning is important for learning higher level information and handling life events.

Using the suggestions in Chapter 8 of Birsh and Carreker (2018) as a starting point, describe how Abraham's weaknesses in cognitive flexibility may hamper his success in various academic subjects, and brainstorm teaching and learning strategies that might be helpful in each academic area.

_____

_____

_____

_____

_____

_____

_____

_____

Executive Function
Metacognition and Self-Regulation

Monica Gordon-Pershey

The processes of cognitive flexibility and inhibitory control allow learners to screen out internal and environmental distractions and maintain task focus. Some learners perform very well on tasks that hold their interest, but they have difficulty putting their own interests aside to focus on academic tasks. Micah, age 9, is a highly verbal child who has several keen interests: electronic gaming, playing guitar, learning how to play tennis, and woodworking. His parents and teachers are impressed by his spatial, motor, and artistic skills and his ability to verbally describe his interests. However, he struggles with the mechanics of literacy, including keeping up with the grade-level curriculum in phonics and spelling and learning how to use punctuation and other print conventions. Micah needs to improve his cognitive flexibility so that he can apply his verbal abilities to these language-based learning demands and maintain the inhibitory control to perform tasks that are outside of his sphere of interest. Metacognitive skills and self-regulation are other areas of executive functioning that Micah can work to improve.

Micah may present a diagnostic conundrum. Diagnostic testing might explore whether he is prone to cognitive interference and/or selective attention. Brainstorm additional ways that psychometric testing might uncover the reasons for the weaknesses in Micah's literacy skills.

_____

_____

_____

Adult supports are important for Micah. How can teachers guide Micah to understand "what to learn" and to show that he has learned it? How can Micah achieve a balance between initiation and inhibition of his thoughts and actions? Describe in detail how the ability to use language to govern learning might be a factor in Micah's situation. Describe how Micah's challenges are related to both executive functioning and language, and explain how the strategies given in Chapter 8 of Birsh and Carreker (2018) can be applied to improve Micah's academic performance.

_____

_____

_____

_____

_____

_____

ACTIVITY 25

Reading Patterns

Some letters have more than one frequent pronunciation. How to pronounce a letter with more than one sound may be determined by the position of the letter in a word and/or the occurrence of the letter with other letters (Carreker, 2018a; Cox, 1992). You will discover that patterns for five letters have more than one frequent pronunciation. Read the words below that contain the same letter. There are multiple pronunciations for the letter. How do you know which pronunciation to use? Decide the pattern that dictates the pronunciation of each letter, and write the pattern. The first pattern is done for you.

PATTERN 1

When is *c* pronounced /k/, and when is *c* pronounced /s/?

cat	cent
cycle	clasp
cup	cot
city	crib

c is pronounced /k/   *before a, o, u, or any consonant* _____

c is pronounced /s/ _____

PATTERN 2

When is *g* pronounced /g/, and when is *g* pronounced /j/?

gate	glad
gypsy	gist
gum	gym
gem	got

g is pronounced /g/ _____

g is pronounced /j/ _____

PATTERN 3

When is *n* pronounced /n/, and when is *n* pronounced /ng/?

nap	snip
sink	sanctuary
finger	vanquish
angle	spin

n is pronounced /n/ _____

n is pronounced /ng/ _____

(continued on next page)

PATTERN 4

When is *x* pronounced /ks/, and when is *x* pronounced /z/?

xylophone	*exit*
expel	*xylem*
xenophobia	*box*
relax	

x is pronounced /ks/ _____

x is pronounced /z/ _____

PATTERN 5

When is *y* pronounced /y/, when is *y* pronounced /ī/, and when is *y* pronounced /ē/?

fly	*reply*	*yellow*
yank	*yield*	*yogurt*
empty	*shy*	*penny*
supply	*Yule*	*happy*

y is pronounced /y/ _____

y is pronounced /ī/ _____

y is pronounced /ē/ _____

Hard and Soft c and g

The letter c can represent the hard sound /k/ or the soft sound /s/. The letter g can represent the hard sound /g/ or the soft sound /j/. Look at the underlined letter in each word below. Check the sounds that the letter represents as hard or soft. Write the pattern that determines that the letter is hard or soft. The first example is done for you.

	Hard	Soft	Pattern
city		✓	*c before i is pronounced /s/*
gem			
clown			
cent			
fancy			
gym			
gist			
space			
energy			
inclusion			
exigent			
facility			
gentleman			
bicycle			
difficult			
registration			
faculty			

Letter Clusters

Label each consonant pair as a *consonant blend*, which retains the individual sounds of each letter, or a *consonant digraph*, which represents one sound.

1. *bl* _____
2. *sh* _____
3. *mp* _____
4. *th* _____
5. *nk* _____

6. *nt* _____
7. *ck* _____
8. *wh* _____
9. *ch* _____
10. *dr* _____

Label each vowel pair as a *digraph*, which consists of two adjacent vowels that represent one sound, or a *diphthong*, which contains two adjacent vowels with a slide or a shift in the middle of the pronunciation.

11. *ea* _____
12. *oi* _____
13. *ou* _____
14. *oe* _____
15. *ai* _____

16. *oy* _____
17. *oo* _____
18. *oa* _____
19. *au* _____
20. *aw* _____

How Many Letters and How Many Graphemes?

TEXTBOOK REFERENCE

Chapters 9 and 20

Letters are symbols. Graphemes are single letters or letter groups that represent specific phonemes or speech sounds. Write the number of letters and the number of graphemes for each word.

		Letters	Graphemes			Letters	Graphemes
1.	bridge	_____	_____	11.	breath	_____	_____
2.	wheel	_____	_____	12.	slant	_____	_____
3.	church	_____	_____	13.	stack	_____	_____
4.	school	_____	_____	14.	shack	_____	_____
5.	show	_____	_____	15.	sketch	_____	_____
6.	band	_____	_____	16.	hand	_____	_____
7.	feet	_____	_____	17.	finish	_____	_____
8.	knife	_____	_____	18.	straw	_____	_____
9.	phone	_____	_____	19.	head	_____	_____
10.	song	_____	_____	20.	shroud	_____	_____

How Many Letters and How Many Graphemes?

TEXTBOOK REFERENCE
Chapters 9 and 20

Letters are symbols. Graphemes are single letters or letter groups that represent specific phonemes or speech sounds. Write the number of letters and the number of graphemes for each word.

		Letters	Graphemes			Letters	Graphemes
1.	deck	_____	_____	11.	teacher	_____	_____
2.	lamp	_____	_____	12.	phone	_____	_____
3.	bench	_____	_____	13.	sports	_____	_____
4.	smoke	_____	_____	14.	plate	_____	_____
5.	glow	_____	_____	15.	stretch	_____	_____
6.	shrine	_____	_____	16.	strand	_____	_____
7.	cheese	_____	_____	17.	clover	_____	_____
8.	pencil	_____	_____	18.	start	_____	_____
9.	state	_____	_____	19.	seed	_____	_____
10.	strong	_____	_____	20.	threat	_____	_____

Vowel Pairs

The adage "When two vowels go walking, the first one does the talking" works about 45% of the time (Adams, 1990). Sort the vowel pairs listed below as those pairs that follow the adage and those pairs that do not.

ai (paint)	ei (vein)	oo (book)
au (saucer)	eu (Europe)	oo (moon)
aw (saw)	ew (pew)	ou (out)
ay (play)	ey (monkey)	ow (show)
ea (teach)	ie (tie)	ow (cow)
ea (head)	ie (priest)	oy (boy)
ea (steak)	oa (boat)	ue (statue)
ee (feet)	oe (toe)	ui (fruit)
ei (ceiling)	oi (oil)	

The first vowel does the talking	The first vowel does not do the talking
ai (paint)	

Vowel-*r* Patterns

When an *r* comes after a vowel, the vowel makes an unexpected sound. Each vowel situation must be taught. Sort the following vowel-*r* patterns by sound.

ar (star), *ar* (dollar), *ar* (warm), *ar* (quart), *er* (fern), *er* (letter), *ir* (first), *ir* (tapir), *or* (fork), *or* (doctor), *or* (work), *ur* (fur), *ur* (murmur)

/er/	/ar/	/or/
ar (dollar)		

Generalizations:

The patterns *er, ir,* and *ur* are always pronounced _____.

In an accented syllable, *ar* is pronounced _____ and *or* is pronounced _____.

In an unaccented syllable, *ar* and *or* are pronounced _____.

After /w/, *or* is pronounced _____.

After /w/, *ar* is pronounced _____.

Syllable Type Definitions

Most words in English can be categorized as one of six syllable types or as a composite of the different syllable types (Carreker, 2018a): closed, open, vowel-consonant-*e*, vowel-*r* (or *r*-controlled), vowel pair (vowel team, vowel combination), and consonant-*le,* which is a type of final stable syllable (Stanback, 1992; Steere, Peck, & Kahn, 1984). Match each syllable type with its correct characteristics.

1. _____ closed syllable

2. _____ open syllable

3. _____ vowel-consonant-*e* syllable

4. _____ vowel pair syllable

5. _____ vowel-*r* syllable

6. _____ consonant-*le* syllable (a kind of final stable syllable)

a. A syllable that has an *r* after the vowel

b. A nonphonetic, recurring syllable that is fairly stable in its pronunciation and spelling

c. A syllable with two adjacent vowels in initial, medial, or final position

d. A syllable that ends in one vowel and at least one consonant

e. A syllable that ends in one vowel

f. A syllable that ends in one vowel, one consonant, and final *e*

Sorting Syllable Types
Closed, Open, Vowel-*r*

Write the words in the appropriate columns, according to the syllable type the word represents. Examples of sorted syllables have been done for you. Refer to Chapter 9 (Carreker, 2018a).

Sort open and closed syllables

hiss   sod   so   hen   he   hem   met   me   west   we

Open	Closed
hi	*hit*

Sort closed and vowel-*r* syllables

firm   car   fond   hand   spur   spun   cat   fork   hard   fist

Closed	Vowel-*r*

Sorting Syllable Types
Closed, Open, Vowel Pairs

Write the words in the appropriate columns according to the syllable type the word represents. Use Chapter 9 (Birsh & Carreker, 2018) as a reference.

Sort closed and vowel pair syllables

miss   seed   toast   help   book   bond   stomp   heap   send   maid

Closed	Vowel pair

Sort open and vowel pair syllables

free   so   fly   deep   mood   be   cry   beet   play   me

Open	Vowel pair

Sorting Syllable Types

Write the following words in the appropriate column. If a word has two syllables, write the word in the two columns that represent the syllable types in the word.

not	here	hive	low	picture	weep
note	her	hi	she	portion	work
nor	hen	hit	sheep	peek	warm
no	mettle	lost	shamble	supreme	my
noon	meet	lone	short	so	mlne
noble	me	lore	shine	soak	marble
he	mean	loan	pie	we	
heat	men	locate	pick	went	

Closed	Open	Vowel-consonant-e	Vowel-r	Vowel pair	Final stable or consonant-le

(continued on next page)

TRY THIS

B   Sorting Syllable Types as a Group Activity

1. Photocopy the Six Syllable Types Chart in Appendix D onto card stock, making one chart.
2. Photocopy the card template on the first page of Appendix E, and cut the chart apart into cards.
3. Distribute the cards to students.
4. Students take turns identifying the syllable types represented on their cards.
5. Students place each card in the appropriate syllable type column on the chart.
6. As students place each card on the chart, they identify the vowel sound in the target syllable, read the word, and use it in an oral sentence.

The second card template in Appendix E can be used separately on another day or can be used with the first card template.

TRY THIS

C   Sorting Syllable Types as an Individual Activity

1. Photocopy the Six Syllable Types Chart in Appendix D onto card stock, making one chart for each student.
2. Photocopy the card template on the first page of Appendix E, and cut the chart apart into cards, making one set for each student. Store each card set in a zip-top plastic bag.
3. Distribute cards and card sets in the bags to students.
4. Students work independently, placing each card in the appropriate syllable type column on the chart.
5. When students have finished sorting their cards, check their work by asking students one at a time to identify the vowel sound in the target syllable, read the word, and use it in an oral sentence. Continue in this manner until all the cards have been checked.

The second card template in Appendix E can be used separately on another day or can be used with the first card template.

Which Syllable Type?

Identify the syllable type of each word or underlined syllable.

1. lump _____

2. smoke _____

3. she _____

4. speech _____

5. clutch _____

6. strict _____

7. thirst _____

8. porch _____

9. stray _____

10. bo<u>ttle</u> _____

11. mon<u>ster</u> _____

12. <u>moi</u>sture _____

13. sim<u>ple</u> _____

14. hun<u>dred</u> _____

15. so<u>lo</u> _____

16. <u>per</u>fect _____

17. ex<u>treme</u> _____

18. pub<u>lish</u> _____

19. cir<u>cle</u> _____

20. <u>fre</u>quent _____

TRY THIS

D   Syllable Types Concentration Game

1. Create a concentration game board using the template in Appendix C.
2. Prepare the game board as an overhead transparency or on an interactive whiteboard.
3. Choose six words or syllables.
4. Write these words or syllables randomly in the empty spaces on the game board.
5. Write the six syllable types that represent each word or syllable randomly in the remaining spaces.
6. Cover each of the squares with small sticky notes.
7. Place the transparency on the overhead projector if using one.
8. Divide students into teams, and determine a rotation.
9. Teams take turns calling out pairs of coordinates (e.g., A3 and B3) to search for a word and a syllable type that match.
10. Uncover the spaces that correspond to the coordinates.
11. If the word and syllable type match, the team gets a point.
12. If the word and syllable type do not match, cover the two spaces again with sticky notes.
13. Each team gets only one turn per round, regardless of whether the team has scored a point.
14. The game continues until all of the spaces have been uncovered.

Generating Syllable Types

Generate 10 examples of each of the syllable types.

Closed_____

_____

_____

Open_____

_____

_____

Vowel-consonant-*e*_____

_____

_____

Vowel pair_____

_____

_____

Vowel-*r*_____

_____

_____

_____

Final stable (e.g., consonant-*le*)_____

_____

_____

(continued on next page)

TRY THIS

E   Syllable Puzzles 1

1. Write the syllables of several two-syllable words on separate index cards. (See Appendix F for sample words.)
2. Lay out two cards that form a two-syllable word in random order.
3. Students take turns identifying the syllable type on each card, identifying the vowel sound in each syllable, and reading the syllables.
4. Students arrange the cards into a word. They read the word and use it in a sentence.

You can also do this activity with three-syllable words. (See the final list included at the end of Appendix F for sample words.)

Syllable Division Patterns

There are four major patterns in English that indicate where a word will be divided into syllables: VCCV, VCV, VCCCV, and V V. The VCCV pattern has two consonants between two vowels. The VCV pattern has one consonant between two vowels. The VCCCV pattern has three consonants between two vowels. The V V pattern has two adjacent vowels that do not represent a vowel digraph or a diphthong.

For each word, identify the syllable division pattern: VCCV, VCV, VCCCV, or V V.

1. mascot   *VCCV* _____
2. rotate _____
3. monster _____
4. bias _____
5. tactic _____
6. cabin _____
7. lion _____
8. supreme _____
9. portray _____
10. second _____

11. pumpkin _____
12. truant _____
13. surround _____
14. instant _____
15. item _____
16. convoy _____
17. instinct _____
18. report _____
19. contrast _____
20. connect _____

Where to Divide
VCCV and VCV Words?

TEXTBOOK REFERENCE

Chapters 9 and 20

There are patterns in English that indicate where a word will be divided into syllables. The two most common patterns are VCCV and VCV. The VCCV pattern has two consonants between two vowels. A word with this pattern is usually divided between the two consonants but can also be divided after the first vowel. The VCV pattern has one consonant between two vowels. A word with this pattern is usually divided before the consonant but can also be divided after the consonant.

Write each word on the line. Divide the word into syllables.

1.	chipmunk	*chip munk*	11.	party
2.	lotus		12.	provide
3.	distance		13.	local
4.	pigment		14.	stubborn
5.	entice		15.	below
6.	banner		16.	market
7.	duty		17.	locate
8.	detain		18.	copper
9.	escape		19.	relate
10.	baby		20.	ribbon

Visit http://library.neuhaus.org/lessonets/syllable-division-review-vccv-words and http://library.neuhaus.org/lessonets/syllable-division-review-vcv-words for lessons on the VCCV and VCV syllable division patterns, respectively.

Where to Divide VCCCV and V V Words?

The four patterns in English for dividing words into syllables are: VCCV, VCV, VCCCV, and V V.

- The VCCCV pattern has three consonants between two vowels. A word with this pattern is usually divided after the first consonant but can also be divided after the second consonant.

- The V V pattern has two adjacent vowels that do not represent a vowel digraph or diphthong, or pronouncing the adjacent vowels as a digraph or diphthong does not produce a recognizable word (e.g., st*oi*c vs. stō/ĭc). A word with this pattern is divided between the two vowels.

Write each word on the line. Divide the word into syllables.

1. chaos   *cha os* _____
2. lion   _____
3. district   _____
4. poem   _____
5. extreme   _____
6. construct   _____
7. duet   _____
8. destroy   _____
9. pumpkin   _____
10. muskrat   _____

11. partner   _____
12. ruin   _____
13. dual   _____
14. distract   _____
15. bias   _____
16. contract   _____
17. dais   _____
18. truant   _____
19. misspell   _____
20. spectrum   _____

Visit http://library.neuhaus.org/lessonets/syllable-division-review-vcccv-words and http://library.neuhaus.org/lessonets/syllable-division-review-vv-words for lessons on the VCCCV and V V syllable division patterns, respectively.

Accent

In most English words, the accent falls on the first syllable. In some words, the accent falls on the second syllable. The accented syllable makes the mouth open wider. The voice is higher and louder.

Write each of the words below and accent the proper syllable.

1. spi der _____
2. bo a _____
3. pre dict _____
4. con stant _____
5. con trol _____
6. na vy _____
7. qui et _____
8. pas tel _____
9. en ter _____
10. can teen _____

11. sev en _____
12. be cause _____
13. cham ber _____
14. con voy _____
15. tri al _____
16. spec trum _____
17. pump kin _____
18. tri umph _____
19. de cide _____
20. chal lenge _____

Syllable Division
Patterns and Choices

There are four major patterns in English that indicate where a word will be divided into syllables: VCCV, VCV, VCCCV, and V V. For each of these four patterns, there are different choices for division and accent placement.

1. The first choice of each pattern involves the most frequent division with the accent on the first syllable.

2. The second choice of each pattern involves the most frequent division with the accent on the second syllable.

3. The third choice of each pattern usually involves a different division with the accent on the first syllable.

Identify the pattern (VCCV, VCV, VCCCV, or V V) and the choice (first, second, or third).

1.	mascot	*VCCV, first*	
2.	rotate		
3.	monster		
4.	bias		
5.	tactic		
6.	cabin		
7.	lion		
8.	supreme		
9.	portray		
10.	second		

11.	pumpkin	
12.	truant	
13.	surround	
14.	instant	
15.	item	
16.	convoy	
17.	instinct	
18.	report	
19.	contrast	
20.	connect	

TRY THIS F

F   Syllable Puzzles 2

1. Write the syllables of several two-syllable words on separate large cards. See Appendix F for sample words.
2. Distribute cards among students.
3. Students move around the room and match their syllables to form words.
4. When students have matched syllables to form words, each pair identifies the syllables in the word and reads it.
5. As each pair reads its word, the student holding the accented syllable holds his or her card higher.

You can also do this activity with three-syllable words. (See the final list included at the end of Appendix F for sample words.)

Short Vowels in Vowel-*r* Syllables

A vowel in a vowel-*r* pattern usually makes an unexpected sound, as in *fur, for, car, her,* and *dirt.* These words look like closed syllables, and you would expect to pronounce the vowel in each word as a short vowel. However, when each of these words is pronounced, the vowel is not pronounced as a short vowel. The *r* after the vowel makes the vowel make an unexpected sound. Therefore, these words are referred to as vowel-*r* syllables and not as closed syllables. An *r* after the vowel alerts the reader that the vowel in the combination with *r* will be pronounced as /er/, /ar/, or /or/. When will the vowel in a vowel-*r* pattern be pronounced as a short vowel?

1. In words of two or more syllables, if there is a vowel-*rr* pattern, the word will divide between the two *r*'s and the vowel in the vowel-*r* pattern will be pronounced as a short vowel, as in *barrel* or *errand.*

2. In a word of two or more syllables, if there is a vowel-*r*-vowel pattern and the word divides after the *r*, the vowel in the vowel-*r* pattern will be pronounced as a short vowel, as in *perish* or *parable.* (To determine that a word such as *perish* divides after the *r*, the reader has already determined that dividing before the *r* does not produce a recognizable word: /pē' rish/ or /pē rish'/.)

All the following words have vowel-*r* patterns. Write the pronunciation of the vowel in each vowel-*r* pattern. The first two examples have been done for you.

1. m<u>err</u>y   /ĕ/
2. c<u>or</u>n<u>er</u>   /or/, /er/
3. f<u>ir</u>st
4. c<u>arr</u>y
5. v<u>er</u>y
6. s<u>ur</u>vey
7. ch<u>err</u>y
8. <u>err</u>and
9. g<u>ar</u>lic
10. d<u>err</u>ick

11. f<u>err</u>et
12. sh<u>er</u>bet
13. m<u>er</u>it
14. b<u>arr</u>ack
15. h<u>ar</u>ness
16. <u>err</u>or
17. <u>or</u>bit
18. c<u>arr</u>ot
19. <u>ur</u>gent
20. n<u>arr</u>ow

Terms for Decoding

Match the examples with the appropriate terms.

1. _____ -ed

2. _____ -ful

3. _____ igh

4. _____ ou, ow, oi, oy

5. _____ /t/ and /d/

6. _____ st, mp, br, dr

7. _____ pin<u>s</u>

8. _____ eigh

9. _____ ad-

10. _____ port

11. _____ struct

12. _____ m<u>et</u>

13. _____ tip<u>s</u>

14. _____ -ist

15. _____ uni-

16. _____ <u>m</u>et

a. bound morpheme

b. consonant suffix

c. vowel prefix

d. blends

e. trigraph

f. quadrigraph

g. unvoiced suffix -s

h. free morpheme

i. diphthongs

j. inflectional ending

k. cognates

l. onset

m. voiced suffix -s

n. consonant prefix

o. vowel suffix

p. rime

Vowel and Consonant Suffixes

A suffix is a letter or group of letters added to the end of a base word. A suffix that begins with a vowel is referred to as a *vowel suffix*. It is important to be able to identify suffixes because, when a vowel suffix is added to the end of a base word, the spelling of the base word may change. A suffix that begins with a consonant is referred to as a *consonant suffix*. Sort the following suffixes as vowel or consonant suffixes:

-en, -ment, -ful, -ity, -ous, -ness, -less, -able, -ish, -ly, -ist, -ward.

Vowel suffixes	Consonant suffixes
_____	_____
_____	_____
_____	_____
_____	_____
_____	_____
_____	

Inflectional Ending -s

The letter -s after a base word that is a verb represents an inflectional ending. For purposes of decoding, this ending acts as a suffix that is added to a base word and indicates the third person singular. The inflectional ending -s has two different pronunciations, /s/ or /z/. After an unvoiced speech sound, it is pronounced /s/. After a voiced speech sound, it is pronounced /z/. Place a check mark in the column corresponding to the correct pronunciation of the ending -s—/s/ or /z/—for each of these derivatives.

		/s/	/z/
1.	seems	_____	_____
2.	jumps	_____	_____
3.	lands	_____	_____
4.	starts	_____	_____
5.	lists	_____	_____
6.	picks	_____	_____
7.	likes	_____	_____
8.	settles	_____	_____
9.	copes	_____	_____
10.	spells	_____	_____
11.	camps	_____	_____
12.	distributes	_____	_____
13.	recycles	_____	_____
14.	screams	_____	_____
15.	grasps	_____	_____

Inflectional Ending -ed

The letters -ed after a base word represent an inflectional ending. For the purposes of decoding, this ending acts as a suffix that is added to a base word and indicates the past tense. The inflectional ending -ed has three different pronunciations, /ĕd/, /t/, or /d/. After the letters t or d, the ending is pronounced /ĕd/. After an unvoiced sound, the ending is pronounced /t/. After a voiced sound, the ending is pronounced /d/. Place a check mark in the column corresponding to the correct pronunciation of ending -ed for each of these derivatives.

	/ĕd/	/t/	/d/
1. seemed	_____	_____	_____
2. jumped	_____	_____	_____
3. landed	_____	_____	_____
4. started	_____	_____	_____
5. tossed	_____	_____	_____
6. picked	_____	_____	_____
7. listed	_____	_____	_____
8. settled	_____	_____	_____
9. copied	_____	_____	_____
10. spelled	_____	_____	_____
11. camped	_____	_____	_____
12. distributed	_____	_____	_____
13. recycled	_____	_____	_____
14. enclosed	_____	_____	_____
15. realized	_____	_____	_____

Inflectional and Derivational Suffixes

Inflectional suffixes are added to a base word or root and create a new word that is the same part of speech as the base word. Derivational suffixes are added to a base word or root and create a new word that is different from the base word in terms of part of speech or function (Moats, 1995, 2010). Derivational suffixes change the meaning, form, or usage of the base word.

Write the part of speech of each base word. Write the part of speech of each derivative. Write the ending or suffix that was added to the base word. Mark whether the suffix is an inflectional or derivational suffix.

Base word	Part of speech	Derivative	Part of speech	Ending or suffix	Inflectional	Derivational
desk	*noun*	desks	*noun*	-s	✓	
help		helpless				
big		bigger				
mow		mowing				
play		playful				
sky		skies				
love		lovely				
small		smallest				
gentle		gentleness				
slow		slower				
merry		merriment				

ACTIVITY 49

Irregular Words for Reading

TEXTBOOK REFERENCE

Chapter 9

Irregular words contain orthographic patterns whose pronunciations do not match the most frequent pronunciations for those patterns. For each word listed, circle the orthographic representation whose pronunciation does not match the most frequent pronunciation.

1. sh(oe)

2. country

3. busy

4. ghost

5. lamb

6. said

7. does

8. doubt

9. four

10. ocean

11. enough

12. aisle

13. friend

14. plaid

15. from

16. would

17. two

18. colonel

Regular or Irregular for Reading?

Words that follow the reliable sound–spelling patterns of the language are regular. Words that do not follow the reliable sound–spelling patterns are irregular. Read each word and mark it with *R* for regular or *I* for irregular.

1. done _____
2. down _____
3. one _____
4. tone _____
5. again _____
6. paint _____
7. seed _____
8. seat _____
9. came _____
10. come _____

11. lose _____
12. lone _____
13. back _____
14. buy _____
15. pretty _____
16. plenty _____
17. become _____
18. began _____
19. any _____
20. orange _____

TRY THIS G

G   Irregular Word Procedure

1. Write an irregular word on the board.
2. Students identify the syllable type and code the word according to the regular patterns of reading. Students read the word and discover it does not follow the reliable patterns of the language.
3. Erase the coded word and rewrite the word on the board. Beside the word, write the pronunciation in parentheses.
4. Students compare the word and the pronunciation and decide which part is irregular.
5. Circle the irregular part.
6. Write the word on the front of a 4" × 6" index card. On the back of the card, write the pronunciation. Cut off the upper left-hand corner of the front of the card. The irregular shape of the card cues students that the word printed on it is an irregular word.
7. Hold up the card so that students see the front of the card. Students read the word aloud.
8. Turn the card around. Students read the pronunciation aloud.
9. Slowly turn the card from front to back four or five times as students read the word and then read the pronunciation aloud.
10. Add the card to a deck of irregular words that is reviewed daily.

Regular or Irregular for Reading?

Read each word and mark it with *R* for regular sound-spelling pattern or *I* for irregular sound-spelling pattern.

1. couch _____

2. some _____

3. whose _____

4. could _____

5. sole _____

6. soul _____

7. eye _____

8. many _____

9. trust _____

10. truth _____

11. debt _____

12. dead _____

13. people _____

14. queen _____

15. between _____

16. together _____

17. trouble _____

18. tremble _____

19. woman _____

20. were _____

21. should _____

22. where _____

23. why _____

24. match _____

Consonant Phonemes

Place of Articulation

When students are aware of the visual display and kinesthetic feel of phonemes, they can identify phonemes in a word and clarify phonemes that are similar (Carreker, 2018a; Moats 1995, 2010; Soifer, 2018). The place of articulation is the place where the flow of air is blocked or changed during production of a consonant sound. Write the following consonant sounds in the appropriate column according to the place of articulation.

/b/   /ch/   /d/   /f/   /g/   /h/   /j/   /k/   /l/   /m/   /n/   /ng/

/p/   /r/   /s/   /sh/   /t/   /th/   /<u>th</u>/   /v/   /w/   /y/   /z/   /zh/

Both lips	Teeth and lower lip	Between the teeth	Ridge behind the teeth	Roof of the mouth	Back of the mouth	From the throat

Consonant Phonemes
Blocked, Partially Blocked, and Unblocked

The terms *blocked*, *partially blocked*, and *unblocked* are used in decoding and spelling instruction to refer to the kinesthetic feel of the position of the tongue, teeth, and lips during the production sounds in isolation (Carreker, 2018a, 2018b). In decoding instruction, *blocked* refers to the steady position of the tongue, teeth, or lips during the entire production of a sound. *Partially blocked* refers to a released position of the tongue or lips during the production of a sound. *Unblocked* refers to no obstruction of the sound by the tongue, teeth, or lips during the production of sounds. These terms are used to aid students in clearly feeling and distinguishing sound.

Sort the consonant sounds below as *blocked*, *partially blocked*, or *unblocked*.

/b/   /ch/   /d/   /f/   /g/   /h/   /j/   /k/   /l/   /m/   /n/   /ng/

/p/   /r/   /s/   /sh/   /t/   /th/   /<u>th</u>/   /v/   /w/   /y/   /z/   /zh/

Blocked	Partially blocked	Unblocked

ACTIVITY 54

Consonant Phonemes
Continuant and Clipped

TEXTBOOK REFERENCE
Chapters 6, 10, and 20

Some consonant sounds are *continuants* and are prolonged in their production, such as /m/ and /n/. Some consonant sounds are *stop sounds* and are obstructed at the place of articulation and are not prolonged in their production, such as /t/ and /p/. During classroom instruction, it is important to clip these stop consonant sounds to prevent the addition of the /uh/ at the end of the sound. These stop sounds are also referred to as *clipped* sounds (Carreker, 2018b). Look at these consonant sounds and determine if in their production they are continuant or clipped. Write *continuant* or *clipped* to the right of each sound.

1. /t/ _____

2. /m/ _____

3. /p/ _____

4. /n/ _____

5. /s/ _____

6. /l/ _____

7. /j/ _____

8. /b/ _____

9. /g/ _____

10. /v/ _____

11. /y/ _____

12. /r/ _____

13. /z/ _____

14. /d/ _____

Multisensory Teaching of Basic Language Skills Activity Book, Fourth Edition   ✳   57

Consonant Phonemes
Cognates

Cognate phonemes have the same visual display, mouth position, and place of articulation (Carreker, 2018b). The only difference is that one sound activates the vocal cords (voiced) and one does not (unvoiced). For example, /ch/ and /j/ are cognates. When you produce these sounds, the visual display, mouth position, and place of articulation are the same. The difference is that your vocal cords are activated when you produce /j/ as in *jeep* (a voiced phoneme) and are not activated when you produce /ch/ as in *cheep* (an unvoiced phoneme). Write the cognates to each phoneme.

Unvoiced	Voiced
/ch/	/j/
/t/	
/f/	
/k/	
/p/	
/s/	
/sh/	
/th/	

Partial or Complete Phonetic Representation for Spelling

The young child's use of invented spelling provides considerable insight as to how well the child is learning and internalizing information about the language (Read, 1971). The child applies his or her phonological awareness and acquired knowledge of sounds and patterns to the task of spelling an unfamiliar word. Look at the invented spellings below and decide whether the spellings represent partial or complete phonetic representation. Write *partial* or *complete*.

1. *st* for *seat* _____
2. *kat* for *cat* _____
3. *ct* for *seat* _____
4. *gv* for *give* _____
5. *whl* for *while* _____
6. *jumpt* for *jumped* _____
7. *rede* for *read* _____
8. *yl* for *while* _____
9. *sop* for *soap* _____
10. *plez* for *please* _____
11. *sep* for *step* _____
12. *pik* for *pick* _____
13. *mn* for *man* _____

14. *moshun* for *motion* _____
15. *teme* for *team* _____
16. *cutry* for *country* _____
17. *hav* for *have* _____
18. *samd* for *seemed* _____
19. *batel* for *battle* _____
20. *enuf* for *enough* _____
21. *lafent* for *elephant* _____
22. *selebr8* for *celebrate* _____
23. *site* for *city* _____
24. *split* for *splint* _____
25. *sd* for *said* _____
26. *wun* for *one* _____

Identifying Spelling Patterns

Write the sound that is represented with the underlined letter or letters and the pattern that determines the use of the letter or letters to represent that sound. Use Chapter 10 in Birsh and Carreker (2018) for reference.

		Sound	**Spelling pattern**
1.	empl<u>oy</u>	/oi/	final /oi/ is spelled oy
2.	gr<u>ou</u>nd		
3.	<u>g</u>iant		
4.	gr<u>ee</u>n		
5.	ma<u>tch</u>		
6.	tun<u>a</u>		
7.	p<u>o</u>lite		
8.	<u>c</u>andy		
9.	lila<u>c</u>		
10.	ugl<u>y</u>		
11.	por<u>ch</u>		
12.	sh<u>y</u>		
13.	w<u>a</u>sp		
14.	blo<u>ck</u>		
15.	do<u>dge</u>		
16.	s<u>k</u>ill		
17.	tr<u>ay</u>		
18.	fl<u>ee</u>		

Five Spelling Rules

A rule word is spelled the way it sounds, but certain information needs to be considered before the word is written. A letter may need to be doubled, dropped, or changed.

Two rules help the speller know when to double a letter in base words:

1. The Rule for Doubling the Final Consonant (the Floss Rule) states that if a one-syllable word ends in /f/, /l/, or /s/ after a short vowel, the final *f, l,* or *s* is doubled.

2. The Rule for Doubling the Medial Consonant (the Rabbit Rule) states that if there is one medial consonant sound after a short vowel in a two-syllable word, the medial consonant is doubled.

Three rules help the speller know when to double, drop, or change a letter at the end of a base word before adding a suffix:

1. The Doubling Rule states that if a base word ends in one vowel, one consonant, and one accent, the final consonant is doubled before adding a vowel suffix.

2. The Dropping Rule states that if a base word ends in final *e,* the *e* is dropped before adding a vowel suffix.

3. The Changing Rule states that if a base word ends in one consonant before a final *y,* the *y* is changed to *i* before adding a suffix that does not begin with *i.*

Match the words with the spelling rule that each exemplifies.

1. _____ better
2. _____ omitted
3. _____ thrill
4. _____ happiness
5. _____ determining

a. The Rule for Doubling the Final Consonant (the Floss Rule)

b. The Rule for Doubling a Medial Consonant (the Rabbit Rule)

c. The Doubling Rule

d. The Dropping Rule

e. The Changing Rule

Go to http://library.neuhaus.org/webinars/five-spelling-rules to view a webinar on the five spelling rules.

Rule Words

For each word listed, write the base word, the suffix, and the spelling rule that is illustrated with each base word or derivative. Use Chapter 10 in Birsh and Carreker (2018) for reference.

		Base word	**Suffix**	**Rule**
1.	hills	_____	_____	_____
2.	letters	_____	_____	_____
3.	swimmer	_____	_____	_____
4.	happiness	_____	_____	_____
5.	racer	_____	_____	_____
6.	dresses	_____	_____	_____
7.	reddish	_____	_____	_____
8.	beginning	_____	_____	_____
9.	penniless	_____	_____	_____
10.	muffins	_____	_____	_____
11.	engaging	_____	_____	_____
12.	omitted	_____	_____	_____
13.	plentiful	_____	_____	_____
14.	enticing	_____	_____	_____
15.	settled	_____	_____	_____
16.	emptied	_____	_____	_____
17.	preferred	_____	_____	_____
18.	permitted	_____	_____	_____

Checkpoints for the Doubling Rule

The Doubling Rule assists students in adding suffixes to base words. When a base word ends in 1) one vowel, 2) one consonant, and 3) one accent, and 4) a vowel suffix is being added, the final consonant is doubled before adding the suffix. If any one of the four checkpoints is missing, the final consonant is not doubled. Look at each base word and the suffix that is to be added. Mark the checkpoints that are present. Write the derivative. If all four checkpoints are present, double the final consonant when writing the derivative.

	One vowel	One consonant	One accent	Vowel suffix	Derivative
hot + est					
run + er					
star + ing					
cup + ful					
steep + est					
stand + ing					
camp + er					
child + ish					
art + ist					
open + er					
begin + er					
benefit + ed					
omit + ed					
travel + ing					
forget + able					

(continued on next page)

TRY THIS

H   Four-Leaf Clover

1. Photocopy the four-leaf clover in Appendix I on green card stock, and cut the clover apart.
2. Laminate the pieces, and affix a magnet to the back of each piece.
3. Place the pieces in random order at the top of a magnetic board.
4. Write the following formulas one at a time on the board.

   hot + est = sip + ed =
   run + er = look + ing =
   swim + ing = slip + er =
   shop + ed = begin + er =
   cup + less = open + ing =
   camp + er = omit + ed =

5. For each formula, students look for the checkpoints for the Doubling Rule (see Activity 60). As students discover each checkpoint, place the pieces of the clover near the formula. If students find all four checkpoints, the final consonant will be doubled. Write the derivative with the doubled final consonant on the board after the equal sign of the appropriate formula. If any one of the checkpoints is missing, the final consonant will not be doubled; write the derivative without the doubled final consonant on the board at the end of the appropriate formula.

Analyzing Words for Spelling

Analyzing words for spelling heightens students' phonemic awareness and orthographic awareness because the students must first determine the sounds in a word and then match the spelling of those sounds in the word. If the sounds are represented by recurring sound–spelling patterns, the word is a regular word. If the sounds are represented by recurring sound–spelling patterns and there is a letter that is doubled, dropped, or changed, the word is a rule word. If the sounds are represented by unexpected orthographic patterns, the word is an irregular word (Carreker, 1992, 2018a).

The words *enough* and *said* are examples of irregular spelling words that contain sound–spelling patterns that are not reliable. Using reliable sound–spelling patterns of the language, one would expect to spell these words *enuf* and *sed*. When reading, one would not be able to sound out the words *enough* and *said*. Therefore, these words are irregular for reading and spelling and must be memorized. However, words that contain less frequent but reliable patterns may be regular for reading but irregular for spelling. For example, in the word *head*, /ĕ/ is spelled *ea*. When the reader encounters this word in reading, he or she will have little difficulty reading the word because a frequent pronunciation of *ea* is /ĕ/. So, the word is regular for reading.

Spelling is a different situation. The most frequent spelling of /ĕ/ is *e*. There is no way to determine when to use *e* and when to use *ea*. The speller must count on frequency. Because *e* is a more frequent spelling, it is the regular, reliable pattern of spelling /ĕ/. Words that contain *ea* to represent /ĕ/ are irregular for spelling although they are regular for reading. Students must memorize these words.

Sort the following words for spelling as regular words, rule words, or irregular words: *batting, pitch, homerun, runner, glove, one, three, nothing, slider, shortstop, player, season, manager, strike, foul*. For each irregular word, underline the part that is irregular.

Regular	Rule	Irregular
_____	_____	_____
_____	_____	_____
_____	_____	_____
_____	_____	_____
_____	_____	_____
_____	_____	_____
_____	_____	_____
_____	_____	_____

Regular, Rule, Irregular for Spelling

Regular words are spelled the way they sound. Regular words do not need to be memorized. *Rule* words are spelled the way they sound, but there is a letter that needs to be doubled, dropped, or changed. Other than the rule that needs to be applied as the words are written, rule words do not need to be memorized. *Irregular* words are spelled in an unexpected way and must be memorized. By analyzing spelling words, students know which words need to be memorized and which ones do not need to be memorized. Analyzing spelling words also calls students' attention to the phonemes and orthographic patterns in words.

Sort the following words as regular words, rule words, or irregular words: *banana, cherry, raspberry, lime, orange, grape, kiwi, strawberry, apple, pineapple, pear, coconut.* For each irregular word, underline the part that is irregular.

Regular	Rule	Irregular
_____	_____	_____
_____	_____	_____
_____	_____	_____
_____	_____	_____

Sort the following words as regular, rule, or irregular: *ocean, sand, swimmer, water, sunning, lifeguard, swordfish, jellyfish, starfish, seaweed, waves, diving.* For each irregular word, underline the part that is irregular.

Regular	Rule	Irregular
_____	_____	_____
_____	_____	_____
_____	_____	_____
_____	_____	_____

Regular or Irregular for Reading and Spelling

When students understand the orthographic patterns of English, they know how to approach words for reading and spelling. The patterns for reading enable students to translate an orthographic representation into a pronunciation. The patterns for spelling enable students to translate a pronunciation into an orthographic representation. A word that is regular for reading (i.e., an expected pronunciation based on the orthographic pattern) may not be regular for spelling (i.e., an expected orthographic representation based on the pronunciation). Look at the words below. Using your knowledge of orthographic patterns, determine whether the words are regular or irregular for reading and regular or irregular for spelling. The first example is done for you. For reading, the orthographic pattern *spĕnd* produces an expected pronunciation, /spĕnd/. For spelling, the pronunciation /spend/ produces the expected orthographic representation, *spend*. Refer to Chapter 10 (Birsh & Carreker, 2018).

		Reading		Spelling	
		Regular	Irregular	Regular	Irregular
1.	spend	✓	_____	✓	_____
2.	said	_____	_____	_____	_____
3.	have	_____	_____	_____	_____
4.	stroke	_____	_____	_____	_____
5.	arbor	_____	_____	_____	_____
6.	weight	_____	_____	_____	_____
7.	soon	_____	_____	_____	_____
8.	get	_____	_____	_____	_____
9.	bus	_____	_____	_____	_____
10.	relive	_____	_____	_____	_____

Planning Lessons for Spelling

Use Chapters 10 and 18 in Birsh and Carreker (2018) for reference and plan 5 days of spelling activities.

Spelling

Day 1	Day 2	Day 3	Day 4	Day 5

Continuous Manuscript Handwriting

The use of continuous manuscript handwriting allows for more fluid movement without the need to lift the pencil during the formation of a letter. Knowledge of correct letter formations facilitates the legibility and speed of handwriting. The use of stroke descriptions aids students in forming letters correctly.

Write the manuscript form of each letter on the line immediately to the right of the printed letter. Match the stroke descriptions with the appropriate letter.

1. b _____

2. m _____

3. l _____

4. s _____

5. z _____

6. d _____

7. e _____

8. v _____

9. o _____

10. i _____

11. c _____

12. w _____

a. Across, around, stop.

b. Slant down, up, down, up.

c. Down, up, around.

d. Around, stop.

e. Curve, slant, curve.

f. Down, hump, hump.

g. Slant down, slant up.

h. Across, slant, across.

i. Down, dot.

j. Around, close.

k. Around, up, down.

l. Down.

Stroke descriptions from Carreker, S. (2002). *Reading readiness* (Handwriting section, p. 1). Bellaire, TX: Neuhaus Education Center; reprinted by permission.

Approach Strokes for Cursive Letters

Cursive lowercase letters can be grouped by four approach strokes: *Swing up, stop; Push up and over; Curve under, over, stop;* and *Curve way up, loop left*. Write the lowercase form of each cursive letter of the alphabet according to its approach stroke. See Chapter 11 in Birsh and Carreker (2018) for further discussion of cursive approach strokes.

Swing up, stop.

Push up and over.

Curve under, over, stop.

Curve way up, loop left.

Approach stroke diagrams courtesy of Luke Waites Center for Dyslexia and Learning Disorders. Texas Scottish Rite Hospital for Children, Child Development Division. (1996). *Teaching cursive writing* [Brochure]. Dallas, TX: Author; reprinted by permission.

Cursive Handwriting Stroke Descriptions

Write the cursive form of each letter on the line immediately to the right of the printed letter. On the line to the right of each cursive form, write the letter that corresponds with the matching stroke description. Note that stroke descriptions can vary (e.g., more or fewer words). The idea is to give students verbal support for forming the letters.

1. i _____ _____
2. e _____ _____
3. l _____ _____
4. t _____ _____
5. c _____ _____
6. x _____ _____
7. a _____ _____
8. s _____ _____
9. j _____ _____
10. h _____ _____
11. m _____ _____
12. o _____ _____

a. Swing way up, pull straight down, release, cross.

b. Curve up and over, stop, trace back around and close.

c. Swing up, loop left, pull straight down, release.

d. Swing way up, loop left, pull straight down, release.

e. Swing way up, loop left, pull straight down, push up and over, pull straight down, release.

f. Curve up and over, stop, trace back, down around, release.

g. Swing up, stop, pull way down straight, loop left, curve up and over, dot.

h. Push up and over, slant down, release, slant down left.

i. Swing up, stop, pull straight down, release, dot.

j. Curve up and over, stop, trace back down around and close, pull straight down, release.

k. Swing up, stop, curve down around, close, release.

l. Push up and over, pull straight down, stop, push up and over, pull straight down, stop, push up and over, pull straight down, release.

Handwriting Practice

Handwriting instruction needs to be explicit and systematic (Wolf & Berninger, 2018). It is brief but regular and focused. As students learn the names and sounds of letters, they connect that information kinesthetically by writing the letters.

Handwriting practice begins with a focus on single letters and then progresses to connecting letters in series and words. Students begin with writing letters using large muscle movements and progress to smaller models and proper proportion. Students trace, copy from a near-point model, write letters without a model, and copy from a far-point model. When connecting letters, it is helpful for students first to practice connecting letters that share the same approach strokes. Students should always name the letter(s) before writing.

On the following chart, write the introduction and practice handwriting activities listed below hierarchically. The first five activities that are written on the chart can be used for introduction and practice of a letter. Use Chapter 11 in Birsh and Carreker (2018) for reference.

- Students copy words from the board.

- Students sky write a new letter while looking at a model. The teacher describes the letter strokes.

- Students write letters with attention to proportion.

- Students write a dictated series of letters that share the same approach stroke.

- Students trace a model of the new letter several times with their fingers.

- Students write a dictated series of letters that contain different approach strokes.

- Students trace a model of a new letter with a pencil.

- Students write a new letter from memory.

- Students trace a model of a series of letters that share the same approach stroke.

- Students trace a model of a series of letters that contain different approach strokes.

- Students copy a model of a new letter on paper.

Introduction and practice activities
1.
2.
3.
4.
5.

(continued on next page)

Practice activities
6.
7.
8.
9.
10.
11.

Planning Lessons for Handwriting

Use Chapters 11 and 18 in Birsh and Carreker (2018) for reference and plan 5 days of cursive handwriting activities for the letter *p*. The letters *i, s,* and *t* have been introduced and practiced.

Handwriting

Day 1	Day 2	Day 3	Day 4	Day 5

The Art and Science of Fluency Instruction

Students' difficulties with fluency will be manifested differently. To become fluent, a reader's instruction must meet his or her needs. The following is a case study from Chapter 12, Appendix 12.2 (Birsh & Carreker, 2018). Determine the reader's strengths and weaknesses and appropriate strategies and activities for improving fluency.

Geoffrey, a wiry 11-year-old, scored mid–second-grade on reading measures when he entered our after-school tutoring lab. He was a wild guesser and self-deprecating, full of "No, no, wait." His early schooling had emphasized rereading leveled trade books of children's literature that schools consider motivating, with the stunning result that near the end of second grade, Geoffrey's teachers found out that he could read several books from memory without recognizing their constituent words in any other context. He was referred for special education services.

Geoffrey and his tutor began their work by building his word-recognition foundation: letter sounds (especially vowels), blending, segmenting, word analogies, and syllable patterns. Geoffrey loved the daily word-card practice and charting his increasing speed. Then, his tutor introduced phrase and sentence practice, which resulted in a totally unexpected slowdown. This slowdown was, fascinatingly, the opposite of many other kids', whose reading gets more fluent in context with the support of phrase structure and the flow of sense. Instead, Geoffrey experienced a slowdown when words came together in the continuous flow of text. When he tried speeding up, he became wildly inaccurate.

From Garnett, K. (2018). Fluency in learning to read: Conceptions, misconceptions, learning disabilities, and instructional moves (Appendix 12.2). In J.R. Birsh & S. Carreker (Eds)., *Multisensory teaching of basic language skills* (4th ed., online content). Baltimore, MD: Paul H. Brookes Publishing Co.; reprinted by permission.)

What are Geoffrey's strengths?

_____

_____

_____

_____

_____

_____

_____

_____

_____

_____

_____

_____

(continued on next page)

What are Geoffrey's needs?

_____

_____

_____

_____

_____

_____

_____

_____

_____

What instructional strategies and activities would best improve Geoffrey's fluency?

_____

_____

_____

_____

_____

_____

_____

_____

_____

_____

_____

_____

Measuring Prosody

Chapter 12 of Birsh and Carreker (2018) outlines procedures for measuring reading rate, or how many words are read correctly in 1 minute. Prosody, the flow and expression of students' reading, also can be measured. To make an objective judgment, you can create a prosody rubric with different features to assess. Features of prosody include

- Using correct intonation for text marked by ending punctuation marks

- Pausing at commas

- Grouping words into meaningful units

- Adjusting stress and pitch to reflect comprehension

Points are given for use of correct intonation and pausing that is marked by punctuation. Points are given for phrasing words into meaningful units and for adjusting stress and pitch to reflect comprehension, such as in a dialogue. Decide what features are present in the first 50 words of a passage, and assign a point value for different features. For example, if there are three commas in the first 50 words, the feature recorded as pausing at commas could have a point value of 3, with 1 point for each comma. Ideally, all four features of prosody are measured in a passage, although the point values for the features may vary.

Feature	Point value
Using correct intonation for text marked by ending punctuation marks	
Pausing at commas	
Grouping words into meaningful units	
Adjusting stress and pitch to reflect comprehension	

Look at the passage in Figure 71.1 on the next page. Mark the 50th word with an asterisk. Based on the features in those 50 words, make a rubric with a 10-point total.

(continued on next page)

The Lion and the Wolf

A very old lion had very bad teeth. "Oh," he moaned loudly. "If only I had teeth, I could chew on something to ease my hunger."

But then he remembered his very weak legs that could not carry his weight. "I can't eat anything anyway because I can no longer hunt something to eat."

The lion laid his head on the ground and prepared himself for death.

A wolf who was nearby could not finish his meal. He saw that the lion was in need of help. He took the rest of his meal to the lion.

The lion smelled the meal and lifted his head. "This is most kind of you," he said to the wolf. "We have not always been the best of friends."

"That is true," said the wolf, "but there is no need for you to suffer when I have more than I need."

Figure 71.1. A passage for measuring prosody.

As students read, give points for the features that are present in students' oral reading. A prosody scale is developed that might look like this:

Prosody scale	
9–10 points	Fluent
7–8 points	Nearly fluent
5–6 points	Progressing
3–4 points	Beginning fluency
0–2 points	Not fluent

With a prosody scale, you will have a measure of speed and accuracy (i.e., how many words a student reads correctly per minute) and a measure of prosody (i.e., the quality of the flow with which a student reads).

Terms for Decoding and Fluency

Match each term with the correct definition.

1. _____ synthetic
2. _____ analytic
3. _____ morpheme
4. _____ syllable
5. _____ explicit instruction
6. _____ blend
7. _____ coarticulation
8. _____ fluency
9. _____ exaggerated pronunciation
10. _____ prosody
11. _____ macron
12. _____ breve
13. _____ irregular word
14. _____ digraph
15. _____ diphthong
16. _____ corrective feedback

a. Direct, purposeful instruction

b. The rhythmic flow of oral reading

c. A word with an unexpected pronunciation or spelling

d. A unit of speech

e. Two adjacent letters in the same syllable that represent one sound

f. A diacritical marking for a long vowel

g. Pertaining to parts that build to a whole

h. A meaning unit of language

i. Two or more letters whose sounds flow smoothly together

j. A diacritical marking for a short vowel

k. Two adjacent vowels in the same syllable whose sounds blend together with a slide or shift during production

l. Reading with rapidity and automaticity

m. The overpronunciation of a word to aid memory

n. The overlapping of adjacent sounds when spoken

o. Pertaining to a whole that is broken into constituent parts

p. Immediate teacher response to student performance that is sensitive to the student's level of skill

(continued on next page)

TRY THIS

I | Rapid Word-Recognition Chart

1. Make a photocopy of the Rapid Word-Recognition Chart in Appendix H.
2. Fill the chart with six words that repeat in a different order in each row.
3. Prepare the chart as an overhead transparency or on an interactive whiteboard.
4. Touch and read the words in the first row.
5. Touch the words in the first row as students read them.
6. Start again at the top. Touch the words as quickly possible, working across each row and down the chart, row by row.
7. Time the students for 1 minute.
8. The initial goal is for students to read the chart two times in 1 minute. Eventually, the goal for students in Grades 3 and higher is to read the chart four times in 1 minute.

Dialogues for Understanding Difficulties With Math

Read the following dialogues. Using Appendix N, determine the difficulties with math that are revealed in the dialogues.

Dialogue A

TEACHER: How many months in a year?

SHAWN: I don't know. (*At this, the teacher offers a bit of prompting, and Shawn recites the names of the months in sequence.*)

TEACHER: So, how many months in a year?

SHAWN: Twenty-eight.

TEACHER: How did you get that answer?

SHAWN: My mother told me.

(*The teacher thinks to herself that the current month is February and wonders if this has anything to do with Shawn's response.*)

_____

_____

_____

_____

_____

(continued on next page)

Dialogue B

TEACHER: What is 10 plus 10?

SHAWN: 20.

TEACHER: So, how much is 10 and 9?

SHAWN: 109.

(The astonished teacher repeats the two-question sequence more slowly and deliberately. But still, Shawn insists that 10 and 9 equal 109.)

TEACHER: Does that make sense to you?

SHAWN: *[Confidently]* Yes—I see it in my mind.

_____

_____

_____

_____

_____

Morphemes, Origins, Meanings, and Derivatives

Knowledge of morphemes facilitates decoding and provides a springboard for vocabulary development and spelling (Adams, 1990) and bridges the gap between alphabetic reading and comprehension (Foorman & Schatschneider, 1997). Fill in the missing information.

Morpheme	Origin	Meaning	Derivatives
ang	Latin	bend	
astro	Greek	star	
auto	Greek	self, unaided	
bio	Greek		biology, biodegradable, biography
chron		time	chronicle, chronometer, synchronize
cogn	Latin		recognize, cognitive, metacognition
cred	Latin		creed, incredible, credulous
duct		lead	
fer	Latin	bear	
geo	Greek	earth	
logy	Greek		
manu	Latin	hand	
pop	Latin	people	
rupt		break	
trans	Latin	across	
vac	Latin	empty	
vert, vers	Latin	turn	
vis	Latin		vision, visible, invisible

Roots and Combining Forms

Generate derivatives for each of the roots or combining forms.

ject (to throw)	ped (foot)	spect (to watch)
reject	*pedal*	*spectator*
projector	*pedestrian*	*inspect*

graph (to write, record)	bio (life)	ology (study of)
autograph	*biographic*	*biology*

syn, sym (same)	form (shape)	cur (to go, flow)
synonym	*formation*	*current*

(continued on next page)

nom (to name)	greg (to gather, group)	voc (to call)
nominate	*congregate*	*vocation*

nym (to name)	pod (foot)	cycl (circle)
antonym	*tripod*	*cyclical*

struct (to build)	vis (to see)	meter (measure)
structure	*visit*	*meter*

Visit http://library.neuhaus.org/lessonets/name-derivative to learn how to play *Name That Derivative*.

ACTIVITY 76

Syllables and Morphemes

TEXTBOOK REFERENCE
Chapters 9, 14, and 20

Identify the number of syllables and morphemes in each of the following words.

		Syllables	Morphemes			Syllables	Morphemes
1.	population	_____	_____	10.	river	_____	_____
2.	combination	_____	_____	11.	watermelon	_____	_____
3.	mustang	_____	_____	12.	canine	_____	_____
4.	summertime	_____	_____	13.	dressmaker	_____	_____
5.	thermostat	_____	_____	14.	mercury	_____	_____
6.	bumblebee	_____	_____	15.	countryside	_____	_____
7.	protection	_____	_____	16.	computing	_____	_____
8.	wheelbarrow	_____	_____	17.	kangaroo	_____	_____
9.	ambulance	_____	_____	18.	vegetables	_____	_____

Clues for Identifying Word Origins

The Anglo-Saxon, Latin, and Greek languages greatly influenced written English. Students who understand the history of English have additional strategies for reading and spelling unfamiliar words (Henry, 1988, 2010). Identify the language layer that is characterized by the following letter patterns or word structures. Write *Anglo-Saxon, Latin,* or *Greek*. Use Chapter 14 in Birsh and Carreker (2018) for reference.

1. The consonant pairs *gn, kn,* and *wr*   _____

2. Roots that end in *ct* and *pt*   _____

3. Vowel pairs   _____

4. Initial consonant clusters *rh, pt, pn,* and *ps*   _____

5. Chameleon prefixes   _____

6. Common, everyday words   _____

7. The consonant cluster *ch* pronounced /k/   _____

8. The letters *c, s,* and t pronounced /sh/   _____

9. Medial *y*   _____

10. Consonant digraphs *ch, sh, th,* and *wh*   _____

11. The affixing of roots   _____

12. Compound words   _____

13. Combining forms   _____

14. The affixing of base words   _____

15. The consonant cluster *ph* pronounced /f/   _____

16. The schwa or unstressed vowel sound   _____

Identifying Word Origins

Identify the origin–Anglo-Saxon, Latin, or Greek–of the following words. Use the clues from the previous activity and Chapter 14 in Birsh and Carreker (2018) for reference.

1. scholar _____
2. dislike _____
3. that _____
4. construction _____
5. phonograph _____
6. made _____
7. excellent _____
8. boat _____
9. conductor _____
10. barn _____
11. microscope _____
12. direction _____
13. transport _____
14. symphony _____
15. chloroplast _____

16. hardware _____
17. photograph _____
18. shipyard _____
19. respect _____
20. spatial _____
21. water _____
22. manuscript _____
23. timely _____
24. portable _____
25. heart _____
26. good _____
27. introduction _____
28. transcript _____
29. bread _____
30. bad _____

TRY THIS

J Sorting Words by Origin

1. Write words of Anglo-Saxon, Latin, and Greek origin on separate cards.
2. Have students sort words into three piles based on origin: Anglo-Saxon, Latin, or Greek.

Identifying Word Origins

Identify the origin—Anglo-Saxon, Latin, or Greek—of the following words. Use the clues in Activity 77 and Chapter 14 in Henry (2018) for reference.

1. food _____

2. rhythm _____

3. lotion _____

4. reject _____

5. eruption _____

6. chorus _____

7. thermometer _____

8. gather _____

9. induction _____

10. intersect _____

11. psychology _____

12. rhododendron _____

13. helpless _____

14. napkin _____

15. wait _____

16. destruction _____

17. sympathy _____

18. football _____

19. illegal _____

20. conduct _____

TRY THIS

K   Word Origin Concentration Game

1. Create a concentration game board using the template in Appendix C.
2. Prepare the game board as an overhead transparency or an interactive whiteboard.
3. Choose two words each of Anglo Saxon, Latin, and Greek origin (six words total).
4. Write these words randomly in the empty spaces on the game board.
5. Write the languages of origin that represent the six words randomly in the remaining spaces.
6. Cover each of the spaces with small sticky notes.
7. Place the transparency on the overhead projector.
8. Divide students into teams and determine a rotation.
9. Teams take turns calling out pairs of coordinates (e.g., A3 and B3) to search for a word and an origin that match.
10. Uncover the spaces that correspond to the coordinates.
11. If the word and origin match, the team gets a point.
12. If the word and origin do not match, cover the two spaces again with the sticky notes.
13. Each team gets only one turn per round, regardless of whether the team has scored a point.
14. The game continues until all of the squares have been uncovered.

Syllables and Morphemes

Syllables are speech units of language that contain one vowel sound, can be represented in written language as words or parts of words, and do not necessarily carry meaning (Moats, 1995). Morphemes are meaning-carrying units of written language such as base words, prefixes, suffixes, roots, and combining forms. Identify the number of syllables and morphemes in each of following words.

		Syllables	Morphemes			Syllables	Morphemes
1.	instructor	_____	_____	10.	photographic	_____	_____
2.	autograph	_____	_____	11.	rattlesnake	_____	_____
3.	destruction	_____	_____	12.	marker	_____	_____
4.	salamander	_____	_____	13.	cucumber	_____	_____
5.	unleaded	_____	_____	14.	barbecue	_____	_____
6.	waits	_____	_____	15.	manuscript	_____	_____
7.	interjection	_____	_____	16.	outstanding	_____	_____
8.	bookkeeper	_____	_____	17.	handshake	_____	_____
9.	conjunction	_____	_____	18.	bluebonnet	_____	_____

TRY THIS

L   Word Part Concentration Game

1. Create a concentration game board using the template in Appendix C.
2. Prepare the game board on an interactive whiteboard.
3. Choose six prefixes, suffixes, and/or roots. (See Appendix G for word parts.)
4. Write these word parts randomly in the empty spaces on the game board.
5. Write the meaning of the six word parts randomly in the remaining spaces.
6. Cover each of the spaces with small sticky notes.
7. Display the game board.
8. Divide students into teams and determine a rotation.
9. Teams take turns calling out pairs of coordinates (e.g., A3 and B3) to search for a word part and definition that match.
10. Uncover the spaces that correspond to the coordinates.
11. If the word part and its definition match, the team gets a point.
12. If the word part and its definition do not match, cover the two spaces again with the sticky notes.
13. Each team gets only one turn per round, regardless of whether the team has scored a point.
14. The game continues until all of the spaces have been uncovered.

Semantic Word Webs

Semantic webs or maps help children connect related concepts and other semantic relationships to a word (Carreker, 2004). In the web below, students write the new vocabulary word on the line at the top left and the part of speech of the word as it is used in the passage on the line at the top right. Students discuss how the word will function in the passage. For example, if the new word is an adjective, it will describe a noun. In the center circle, students write the origin and definition of the word. In the upper left-hand circle, students write two or three synonyms for the target word. In the upper right-hand circle, students write two or three antonyms. In the lower left-hand circle, students write words that illustrate the function of the word. If the vocabulary word is an adjective, students write a noun in each lower circle that could be described by the new word. If the vocabulary word is a verb, students write an adverb in each of the lower circles that would describe the verb. If the vocabulary word is a noun, students write an adjective in each circle that could describe the word. Finally, on the line below the web, students write a sentence that demonstrates their understanding of the new word.

Web the word *prevaricate*.

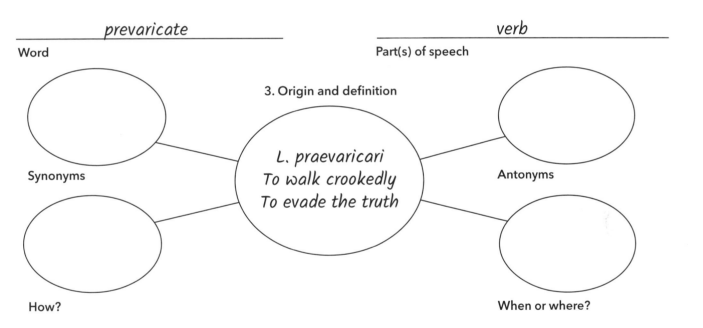

prevaricate

Word

verb

Part(s) of speech

3. Origin and definition

*L. praevaricari
To walk crookedly
To evade the truth*

Synonyms

Antonyms

How?

When or where?

Sentence

Derivative Word Web

A derivative web (Carreker, 2004) is used for words with recognizable, recurring word parts. Students write the new vocabulary word (e.g., *inject*) on the line at the top to the left and the part of speech on the top line at the right. In the center circle, students write the origin, the word parts that make up the word and their meanings, and the definition of the word. In each of the three upper circles, students write a derivative that contains one word part (e.g., three derivatives with prefix *in-* meaning *in* or *into*). In the other three circles, students write three derivatives that contain the other word part (e.g., three derivatives with the root *ject,* meaning *to throw*). Finally, students write a sentence with the word on the line at the bottom of the web. This web is intended to show how learning word parts economizes the learning of new vocabulary and how words with common word parts share a sense of the same meanings.

Web the word *inject*.

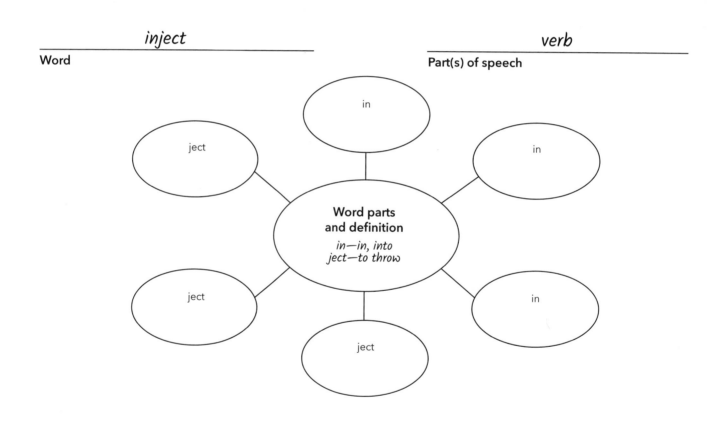

inject	*verb*
Word	**Part(s) of speech**

Word parts and definition

in—in, into
ject—to throw

(circles: in, in, in, ject, ject, ject)

Multiple Meaning Webs

Students use a multiple meaning web (Carreker, 2004) to show multiple meanings of a vocabulary word. They write a word from a passage they are reading on the top left-hand line of the web and in the center circle. Students list possible parts of speech for the word on the top right-hand line. They write six different meanings on the web, one meaning in each circle. Students write a sentence using the meaning that is germane to the passage on the line at the bottom of the web.

Web the word *run*.

run   _verb, noun_

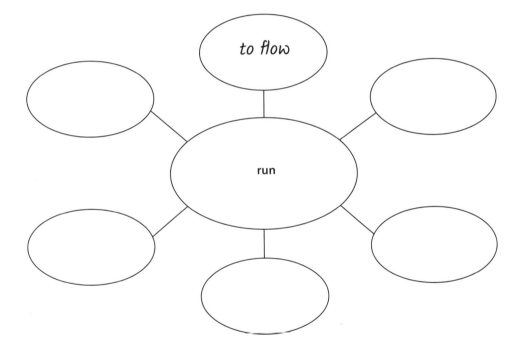

(continued on next page)

TRY THIS

M Semantic Webs

1. Make photocopies of the semantic web template in Appendix J.
2. Students create word profiles for the following words and other words that are appropriate.

(See Activity 81 for instructions on creating semantic webs.)

meadow	versatile
suburb	semantic
gist	antediluvian
exasperate	

TRY THIS

N Derivative Webs

1. Make photocopies of the derivative web template in Appendix J.
2. Students create word profiles for the following words and other words that are appropriate.

(See Activity 82 for instructions on creating derivative webs.)

telephone	manuscript
bicycle	revert
photograph	transport
tripod	

TRY THIS

O Multiple Meaning Webs

1. Make photocopies of the multiple meaning web in Appendix J.
2. Students create word profiles for the following words and other words that are appropriate.

(See Activity 83 for instructions on creating multiple meaning webs.)

run	lap
slip	hand
tip	give
trunk	

Word Profiles

Thorough knowledge of word origins as well as the phonological, orthographic, and morphological aspects of words builds words in memory, making them easier to retrieve. Thorough knowledge of the semantic, syntactic, and pragmatic uses of words increases students' comprehension. This knowledge also supports fluency as skilled readers use their knowledge of word meanings to group words into meaningful units, which aids prosody. The example below shows a word profile. Such a profile heightens students' awareness of all of the aspects of a word. Study this profile, and then create a profile for the word *like*.

Sample Word Profile

Word: _light_

Number of phonemes: _3_

Phonemes: _/l/ / ī / /t/_

Rime pattern: _ight as in fight, might, tight, sight, bright, plight_

Number of letters: _5_

Letters: _l, i, g, h, t_

Number of graphemes: _3_

Graphemes: _l, igh, t_

Spelling pattern(s): _irregular for spelling_

Origin: _Anglo-Saxon_

Derivatives: _lighter, lightly, lightness, lighten_

One definition: _a source of brightness_

Multiple meanings: _not heavy, graceful, sunny, carefree, to ignite_

Synonyms: _glow, weightless, bright, untroubled, set on fire_

Antonyms: _heavy, dark, extinguish_

Part(s) of speech: _noun, adjective, adverb, verb_

Usage (formal or informal): _can be used in formal and informal writing_

Figurative usages: _light as a feather, to make light of, light of my life_

(continued on next page)

Word Profile

Word: *like*

Number of phonemes: _____ Phonemes: _____

Rime pattern: _____

Number of letters: _____ Letters: _____

Number of graphemes: _____ Graphemes: _____

Spelling pattern(s): *Medial / ī/ in a one-syllable base word is spelled i-consonant-e* _____

Origin: _____

Derivatives: _____

One definition: _____

_____

Multiple meanings: _____

_____

Synonyms: _____

_____

Antonyms: _____

Part(s) of speech: _____

Usage (formal or informal): _____

Figurative usages: _____

Word Profiles

Create a word profile for the word *play*. Do not use a dictionary. Think about what you know and have learned about all the domains of language–phonology, morphology, syntax, pragmatics, and orthography.

Word: **play**

Number of phonemes: _____ Phonemes: _____

Rime pattern: _____

Number of letters: _____ Letters: _____

Number of graphemes: _____ Graphemes: _____

Spelling pattern(s): _____

_____

Origin: _____

Derivatives: _____

One definition: _____

_____

Multiple meanings: _____

Synonyms: _____

Antonyms: _____

Part(s) of speech: _____

Usage (formal or informal): _____

Figurative usages: _____

_____

(continued on next page)

TRY THIS

P Word Profiles

1. Make copies of the template in Appendix L.
2. Following the process described in Activities 84 and 85, have students create word profiles for the following words:

tip	run
top	light
lap	like
slip	sink
trunk	rock
box	

Semantic Feature Analysis

Semantic feature analysis helps students learn new vocabulary and see the relationships among concepts, other words, and ideas or information in a text (Hennessey, 2018). A matrix is constructed that shows examples and features of a targeted concept or word. A check mark signifies a relationship, an *X* signifies a nonrelationship, and a question mark shows uncertainty of a relationship. Without looking at the features across the top of the following matrix, write examples of the target concept in the left-hand column. Mark relationships with check marks, nonrelationships with *X*s, and uncertainty with question marks.

Vegetables	Grows in the ground	Grows on a vine	Is yellow or orange	Contains beta-carotene	Is eatable raw	Is considered a crucifer	Has a high starch content

(continued on next page)

In the following matrix, write the definition of *carnivore* in the first square. Fill in features of carnivores across the top. Write examples of carnivores in the left-hand column. Mark relationships with check marks, nonrelationships with *X*s, and uncertainty with question marks.

Carnivores							

TRY THIS

Q Semantic Feature Analysis

1. Make copies of the template in Appendix K.
2. Following the process described in Activity 86, have students create semantic feature analysis matrices for the following concepts:

plant

fruits

trees

animals

reptile

mammals

minerals

transportation

cities

countries

Tiers of Vocabulary Words

Beck, McKeown, and Kucan (2013) outlined different tiers of vocabulary:

- *Tier One* words are common, basic words that are used in everyday conversations and that most children know; these are not usually the target of instruction.

- *Tier Two* words are more sophisticated words often used by mature language users in speech and writing; they are found across a variety of texts and domains.

- *Tier Three* words are words with more narrow and specific roles in language, words that are not necessarily familiar to mature language users.

Categorize the following words by tiers. Refer to Chapter 15 (Birsh & Carreker, 2018).

esophagus	*napkin*	*health*	*euphemism*	*interpret*
hunt	*important*	*rhetoric*	*declare*	*forest*
relate	*erupt*	*dysplasia*	*geriatric*	*knowledge*
protoplasm	*discontent*	*happening*	*featured*	*specific*

Tier One	Tier Two	Tier Three

Student-Friendly Definitions

To introduce new vocabulary words, Beck, McKeown, and Kucan (2013) suggested using student-friendly definitions. These definitions explain the meanings of words in everyday language and provide a familiar context. The definitions are often framed with "someone" or "something" (Hennessy, 2018). Below are vocabulary words and dictionary definitions. The first word is done for you. Create student-friendly definitions for the other words. Use Chapter 15 (Birsh & Carreker, 2018) as a reference.

Word	Dictionary definition	Student-friendly definition
sympathetic[a]	Sympathetic: existing or operating through an affinity, interdependence, or mutual association	*Someone who understands or shares the same feelings or concerns as someone else is sympathetic. For example, even though they are not people, I am sympathetic to abandoned animals who might feel lonely, sad, and afraid.*
vocation[a]	Vocation: a summons or strong inclination to a particular state or course of action	
philosophy[a]	Philosophy: the most basic beliefs, concepts, and attitudes of an individual or group	
inference[a]	Inference: the act of passing from one proposition, statement, or judgment considered as true to another whose truth is believed to follow from that of the former	
exuberant[a]	Exuberant: joyously unrestrained and enthusiastic	

[a]By permission. From *Merriam Webster's Collegiate® Dictionary, 11th Edition* © 2011 by Merriam-Webster, Incorporated (www.merriam-webster.com).

Precision in Use of Vocabulary

As students learn new words, they will discover that many words share the same or almost the same meaning. The meanings of these words may be similar, but they differ in intensity, making some words more appropriate than other words in a given context. The awareness of intensity helps students understand an author's choice of words and helps them make the best choices for their writing. The words listed below mean *unhappy*. Write *L* for less intensive and *M* for more intensive. Refer to Chapter 15 (Birsh & Carreker, 2018).

sullen	_____	disconsolate	_____	despondent	_____	sad	_____
gloomy	_____	cheerless	_____	somber	_____	glum	_____
down	_____	distraught	_____	forlorn	_____	sorrowful	_____
devastated	_____	depressed	_____	discontented	_____	blue	_____
disappointed	_____	dejected	_____	low	_____	pessimistic	_____

Usage

Because of the rain, the picnic was canceled, and the children were _____ but not _____.

The hurricane completely destroyed the town, and the people were not just _____; they were _____.

Generate a gradient list of 20 antonyms for *unhappy*.

_____

_____

_____

_____

_____

_____

_____

_____

_____

_____

_____

_____

Comprehension
Summarization

Summarization requires students to think about what they have read and to identify the most important information (Carreker, 2004; Marzola, 2018). Initially, students strive to summarize a passage in about one third the number of words in a passage. Students ultimately strive to summarize a passage in one fourth the number of words. When students summarize a passage, they make decisions about what information is important and what information is expendable.

Read the passage called "Rhinoceroses" in Appendix M, and write a summary below. The passage has 177 words. Write a summary with one third of the number of words in the passage, or about 59 words.

_____

_____

_____

_____

_____

_____

_____

_____

_____

_____

_____

TRY THIS

R Summarization

1. Photocopy a passage from Appendix M.
2. After students have listened to or read the passage, they write a summary paragraph using one third the number of words in the passage. Serve as scribe if needed.

Comprehension

Text-Dependent
Questions and Summarization

Read the passage called "Georgianna and the Lemonade Stand" in Appendix M, and write 5 text-dependent questions that require the reader to look back at the text for evidence.

1. _____

2. _____

3. _____

4. _____

5. _____

After writing the questions, write two summaries below. The passage has 380 words. Write one summary with one third of the number of words in the passage, or about 127 words. Then, write the second summary paragraph with one fourth the number of words in the passage, or about 95 words.

Summary One

_____

_____

_____

_____

_____

_____

_____

_____

_____

_____

_____

_____

(continued on next page)

Summary Two

_____

_____

_____

_____

_____

_____

_____

_____

_____

_____

_____

_____

Parts of Speech

Grammar and syntax aid students in several ways. Students use their knowledge of grammar and syntax to group words into meaningful phrases as they read. This grouping of words gives reading a rhythmic flow (prosody) that facilitates comprehension. Syntactic knowledge helps students understand how to use new vocabulary words in their oral and written discourse. This knowledge helps students construct sentences as they write.

Instruction begins with the key elements of speech–nouns, pronouns, verbs, adjectives, and the articles *the, a,* and *an.* The other parts of speech are added when students have a firm understanding of the essential elements. Prepositions and adverbs expand sentences by telling how, when, or where. Coordinating conjunctions such as *and* and *or* enable students to combine simple sentences into compound sentences. Interjections add emphasis or emotion.

Look at the following sentences. Under each word, write the part of speech that is represented by the word. You can use abbreviations such as *adj.* for *adjective, adv.* for *adverb, conj.* for *conjunction, interj.* for *interjection, prep.* for *preposition,* and *pron.* for *pronoun.*

1.   Three homes at Fifth Street and Pine burned.

2.   That dog ran home.

3.   The red shirts will run in hot water.

4.   Well, I have another run in my sock.

5.   The play last night was fun.

6.   He left his book on the bus yesterday.

7.   Those students have no time for fun and games.

8.   No, the teacher said we must finish our assignment.

9.   Many children happily played a game.

10.   Two big events are planned for this year.

Syntax

Syntax, the arrangement of sentences, can be introduced or practiced with the use of sentence expansion activities in Chapter 17 (Birsh & Carreker, 2018). Students begin with a core sentence and add elements to it. Use the following prompts to expand the sentence *The birds sang*:

1. Write the sentence, and add an adjective that describes the birds.

   _____

2. Rewrite the previous sentence, and add an adjective and noun that tell what the birds sang.

   _____

3. Rewrite the previous sentence, and add a prepositional phrase that tells where the birds sang.

   _____

4. Rewrite the previous sentence, and add another adjective that describes what the birds sang.

   _____

5. Rewrite the previous sentence, and add an adverb or an adverbial phrase that tells when the birds sang.

   _____

ACTIVITY 94

Composition
The Descriptive Paragraph

Some students benefit from learning to write paragraphs in sentence form. They write sentences that follow the structure of a paragraph's purpose, edit them, and then write them in paragraph form. As students gain proficiency in vocabulary, syntax, and paragraph writing, this formulaic structure yields to more natural expression. Below are structure sentences for a descriptive paragraph.

1. Write a sentence that names the object and its category.
2. Write a sentence that states the function or use of the object.
3. Write a sentence about one characteristic.
4. Write a sentence about another characteristic.
5. Write a sentence that uses a simile or metaphor to compare the object to another object.
6. Write a sentence that restates the first sentence, provides a fact, or offers an opinion.

Write a descriptive paragraph about your hand.

_____

_____

_____

_____

_____

_____

_____

_____

_____

_____

Composition
Writing a Descriptive Paragraph

Look at Figure 95.1. Write six sentences as prescribed below about the picture in Figure 95.1.

Figure 95.1. A picture for writing a descriptive paragraph.

1. Write a sentence that names the object and its category.

   _____

2. Write a sentence that states the function or use of the object.

   _____

3. Write a sentence about one characteristic.

   _____

4. Write a sentence about another characteristic.

   _____

(continued on next page)

5. Write a sentence that uses a simile or metaphor to compare the object to another object.

_____

6. Write a sentence that restates the first sentence, provides a fact, or offers an opinion.

_____

Edit the sentences.

Write the edited sentences in paragraph form on the lines below.

_____

_____

_____

_____

_____

_____

_____

_____

_____

_____

_____

_____

_____

_____

(continued on next page)

TRY THIS

S The Narrative Paragraph

1. Students use the following outline to write a narrative paragraph about the day they discovered a dinosaur in their backyard.

    Sentence 1—State event.
    Sentence 2—State what happens first.
    Sentence 3—State what happens next.
    Sentence 4—State what happens then.
    Sentence 5—State what happens finally.
    Sentence 6—Restate event.

2. Students edit their paragraphs.
3. Students read their paragraphs aloud.

Composition
Writing an Argument Paragraph

An argument paragraph presents a claim, reasons for the claim, and provides evidence that supports the claim. Write an argument paragraph as prescribed below. The topic is "Is daylight savings time necessary?"

1. State your claim.

_____

2. Give a reason for your claim.

_____

3. Cite a piece of evidence that supports your claim.

_____

4. Give a second reason for your claim.

_____

5. Cite a piece of evidence that supports your second reason.

_____

6. Give your most compelling reason for your claim.

_____

7. Cite a piece of evidence that supports your third reason.

_____

(continued on next page)

8. Present a counterclaim.

    _____

9. Restate your claim.

    _____

Edit the sentences.

Write the edited sentences in paragraph form on the lines below.

_____

_____

_____

_____

_____

_____

_____

_____

_____

_____

_____

_____

Composition
The Effortless Paragraph

For students who experience a great deal of difficulty in writing paragraphs, the process can be further simplified with the following procedure.

Look at the image in Figure 97.1. List 10 nouns that are seen in the picture in the *Noun* column of the following chart. Start at the top of the image, and work down to the bottom. After listing the nouns, list one verb in present tense that relates to each noun and the picture. After listing the verbs, list two adjectives for each noun.

Figure 97.1. A picture for writing an effortless paragraph.

Adjective	Adjective	Noun	Verb

(continued on next page)

Write 10 sentences, using one row of information from the chart for each sentence. Add an article, a prepositional phrase, a direct object, or an adverb when constructing your sentences.

1. _____

2. _____

3. _____

4. _____

5. _____

6. _____

7. _____

8. _____

9. _____

10. _____

Edit your sentences. Delete one of the two adjectives that describe each noun. Rearrange words. Insert a word. Are there sentences that could be combined into a complex sentence?

_____

_____

_____

_____

_____

_____

_____

_____

_____

(continued on next page)

Choose six edited sentences. Write them in order below in paragraph form.

_____

_____

_____

_____

_____

_____

_____

_____

_____

_____

Composition
Transition Words and Phrases

The flow of writing is facilitated by the use of transition words (Hochman, 2018). Transition words sequence ideas, emphasize a point, indicate a change in thought, illustrate a point, or draw a thought or idea to a conclusion. Categorize these transitional words: *first, finally, therefore, for example, obviously, yet, above all, before, specifically, thus, in summary, as an illustration, otherwise, certainly, keep in mind*

Time and sequence

_____

_____

_____

Emphasis

_____

_____

_____

Change of direction

_____

_____

_____

Illustration

_____

_____

_____

Conclusion

_____

_____

_____

Planning Lessons for Phonological Awareness, Alphabet Knowledge, and History of Language

TEXTBOOK REFERENCE
Chapters 3, 5, 6, 14, and 18

A daily lesson plan is needed to organize information for presentation (Birsh, Schedler & Singer, 2018). The first day usually is a review or a probe of known skills. The subsequent lessons introduce new information or extend and refine known and new skills. Using the charts provided below, plan 5 days of activities for oral language and phonological awareness, alphabet knowledge, and word origin. Use Chapters 3, 5, 6, and 14 in Birsh and Carreker (2018) for reference.

Oral language and phonological awareness

Day 1	Day 2	Day 3	Day 4	Day 5

(continued on next page)

Alphabet knowledge

Day 1	Day 2	Day 3	Day 4	Day 5

Word origin

Day 1	Day 2	Day 3	Day 4	Day 5

Planning Lessons for Beginning Reading

TEXTBOOK REFERENCE

Chapters 9, 10, and 18

A daily lesson plan organizes information for presentation (Birsh, Schedler, & Singer, 2018). The first day's activity in a weekly lesson often is a review or a probe of known skills. The subsequent days' lessons introduce new information or extend and refine known and new skills. Plan 3 days of new concept introduction and review activities. A review activity and a concept introduction have been planned for you. Plan 4 days of reading practice activities that reinforce known skills. The first reading practice has been planned for you.

For the purposes of planning, assume that the students have learned the short vowels *a* and *i* and the consonants *d, f, g, h, l, n, p, s,* and *t*. The next three letter introductions are short vowel *o* and consonants *m* and *b*. Plan the reviews of previously introduced concepts and the introductions of the new letters and sounds. Decide on which day students will review, on which day you will introduce *m*, and on which day you will introduce *b*. Based on what students know, what words could students read each day? Make a list of 15 words for each day. Use only those letters that have been introduced. Decide if students will read words on the board or on paper or will use letter tiles to make and read words. Introducing new concepts and reading practice activities are explained in Carreker (2018a). Refer to the lesson plan models in Figures 18.3-18.6 in Chapter 18 (Birsh & Carreker 2018).

New concept introduction or review

Day 1	Day 2	Day 3	Day 4	Day 5
Review—students repeat sequences of sounds and blend them into words. For example, /n/ /ă / /p/ /s/ /n/ /ă / /p/ /s/ /p/ /ĭ/ /t/ /s/ /p/ /ĭ/ /n	Introduce short vowel /ŏ/. Discovery words: *off toss* *on soft* *frost* Key word: *octopus*			

Reading practice

Day 1	Day 2	Day 3	Day 4	Day 5
Students will read words on a reading practice page. *hit pats* *hip past* *hiss last* *hips fast* *sip flap* *slip slat* *snip slap* *spin pins*				

Spelling practice

Day 1	Day 2	Day 3	Day 4	Day 5
Students will spell words. *sit* *sip* *pit* *snip* *spit* *list*				

Spanish Phonemes

There are 23 phonemes or speech sounds in Spanish (Barrutia & Schwegler, 1994). In English, there are about 44. Many sounds in Spanish and English directly transfer from one language to the other (Cárdenas-Hagan, 2018). These sounds are *cognates*.

Look at the English sounds below. Check *yes* if there is a cognate in Spanish. Check *no* if there is no cognate. Use Chapter 19 in Birsh and Carreker (2018) for reference.

Cognate in Spanish?

English consonant sound	Yes	No
/m/	_____	_____
/s/	_____	_____
/sh/	_____	_____
/t/	_____	_____
/d/	_____	_____
/j/	_____	_____
/zh/	_____	_____
/k/	_____	_____
/th/	_____	_____

Look at the Spanish sounds below. Check *yes* if there is a cognate in English. Check *no* if there is no cognate.

Cognate in English?

Spanish consonant sound	Yes	No
/rr/	_____	_____
/b/	_____	_____
/ñ/	_____	_____
/p/	_____	_____
/g/	_____	_____
/f/	_____	_____
/ch/	_____	_____
/l/	_____	_____

Reason for Final e

Final *e* at the end of words is almost always silent. Final *e* serves several functions (Wilson, 2018). It is used to make a vowel long or to make *c* or *g* soft. It can be part of a consonant-*le* syllable. Because English words do not end in *v*, *e* is added as the final letter when a word ends in final /v/, and it may or may not influence the vowel sound. In the chart are base words that end in silent *e*. Write in the reason for the final silent *e*, and then form derivatives by adding the indicated endings and suffixes. Use Chapter 20 in Birsh and Carreker (2018) for reference.

Word	Reason for Silent *e*	Derivatives
name		(Add -*ing*, -*ed*, and -*less*.)
shave		(Add -*ing*, -*ed*, and -*er*.)
battle		(Add -*ing*, -*ed*, and -*ment*.)
infringe		(Add -*ing*, -*er*, and -*ment*.)
trace		(Add -*ing*, -*ed*, and -*able*.)

ACTIVITY 103

Creating an
Educational Memories Sample

TEXTBOOK REFERENCE

Chapter 21

An Educational Memories sample (Blumenthal, 1981) records a person's positive and negative memories of his or her educational experience. It can reveal insights that a person has about his or her strengthens and difficulties, how the person has dealt with any difficulties, and the emotional impact of the difficulties. It also provides a writing sample that demonstrates the person's organizational and writing skills. People without learning problems tend to have more positive memories of their educational experiences than those with learning problems (Blumenthal, 2018).

On the lines below, write your memories of your educational experiences.

_____

_____

_____

_____

_____

_____

_____

_____

_____

_____

_____

_____

_____

_____

_____

_____

_____

_____

_____

_____

_____

APPENDIX CONTENTS

Photocopiable and Downloadable Material

Appendix A	Major Research Findings That Support Structured Literacy
Appendix B	Instant Letter-Recognition Chart
Appendix C	Concentration Game Board
Appendix D	Six Syllable Types
Appendix E	Words for Six Syllable Types Chart
Appendix F	Practice Words for Syllable Division
Appendix G	Suffixes, Prefixes, Roots, and Combining Forms
Appendix H	Rapid Word-Recognition Chart
Appendix I	Four-Leaf Clover
Appendix J	Word Webs
Appendix K	Semantic Feature Analysis
Appendix L	Word Profile
Appendix M	Comprehension Passages
Appendix N	Types of Math Deficits
Appendix O	Building Block Checklist for Effective Classroom Management

Major Research Findings That Support Structured Literacy

ORAL LANGUAGE

Long before children begin to read, they need language and literacy experiences at home and in preschool to develop a wide range of knowledge that will support them later in acquiring linguistic skills necessary for reading. These include language play such as saying rhymes, writing messages, listening to and examining books, developing oral vocabulary and verbal reasoning, and learning the purposes of reading. Exposure to reading aloud and oral language play foster development of phonemic awareness.

PHONEMIC AWARENESS

Reading development depends on the acquisition of phonemic awareness and other phonological processes. Phonemic awareness is the ability to understand the sound structure in spoken words. To learn to read, however, children must also be able to pay attention to the sequence of sounds or phonemes in words and to manipulate them. This is difficult because of the coarticulation of the separate sounds in spoken words. Children learn to do this by engaging in intensive oral language activities of sufficient duration, such as identifying and making rhymes, counting and working with syllables in words, segmenting initial and final phonemes, hearing and blending sounds, analyzing initial and final sounds of words, and segmenting words fully before learning to read and during beginning reading. This training facilitates and predicts later reading and spelling achievement.

ALPHABET KNOWLEDGE

It is essential that children learn the alphabet and be able to say the names of the letters, recognize the shapes, and write the letters. These skills are powerful predictors of reading success.

PHONICS

Along with instruction on letter names, children need well-designed and focused phonics instruction to learn letter–sound correspondences. Fast and efficient decoding and word-reading skills rest on this alphabetic principle: how the written spellings of words systematically represent the phonemes in the spoken words. The beginning reader must start to connect the 26 letters of the alphabet with the approximately 44 phonemes in English.

PRACTICE WITH DECODABLE TEXTS

Children need to practice new sounds and letters using materials (i.e., controlled decodable texts) that directly reinforce the new information and that review what children already know for maximum gains in fluency and automaticity.

EXPOSURE TO SIGHT WORDS AND IRREGULAR WORDS

Sight word reading happens when children are able to read words from memory. Repeated exposures build the alphabetic features in memory so words can be read by sight.

It is also important for children to have a store of high-frequency irregularly spelled words so that they can read more than just controlled texts when they are ready.

ACCURATE AND AUTOMATIC WORD RECOGNITION

Fluency and comprehension depend on accurate and automatic word recognition. Slow decoders are poor at comprehension because of reduced attentional and memory resources. Systematic word recognition instruction on common, consistent letter–sound relationships and syllable patterns supports successful word recognition skills.

SPELLING

When children are familiar with the spelling regularities of English, their reading and spelling are strengthened. Opportunities to apply the predictable and logical rules and spelling patterns that match the reading patterns being learned give children a double immersion in the information. Spelling is an essential and interconnected complement to reading instruction.

COMPREHENSION

Comprehension depends on the activation of relevant background knowledge and is related strongly to oral language comprehension and vocabulary growth. Along with explicit vocabulary instruction, metacognitive strategies such as questioning, predicting, making inferences, clarifying misunderstandings, and summarizing while reading should be included in comprehension instruction.

SYSTEMATIC, EXPLICIT INSTRUCTION

Poor readers need highly systematic, structured, explicit, and intensive one-to-one or small-group instruction that recognizes their developmental level in phonemic awareness, word recognition, and comprehension processes. Implicit instruction has been found to be counterproductive with children with learning disabilities or children at risk for not learning to read and produces fewer gains in word recognition and decoding skills than does explicit, intensive instruction based on systematic phonics.

WELL-TRAINED TEACHERS

Well-trained, accomplished teachers who can analyze instruction and monitor progress, set goals, and continue to learn about effective practices are the mainstay of children's success in learning to read.

Instant Letter-Recognition Chart

Concentration Game Board

	1	2	3	4
A				
B				
C				

Six Syllable Types

Closed	Open	Vowel-consonant-e	Vowel-r	Vowel pair	Final stable syllable

Words for Six Syllable Types Chart

and	him	he	five	seem	first	candle	nation
got	not	she	cake	look	fern	scramble	nature
cub	get	go	rope	need	fork	uncle	mention
fast	plant	hi	cube	paint	far	noodle	adventure
run	splint	so	these	boat	fur	steeple	explosion
met	clock	no	cape	each	third	bottle	invention
send	strand	me	line	spoon	mark	ruffle	erosion
hen	blank	be	note	spoil	short	puzzle	capture

Words for Six Syllable Types Chart

end	top	tub	list	gum	hand	leg	sent
milk	hot	hunt	split	slant	block	grand	shrank
locate	baby	lilac	sofa	fever	noble	even	belong
strike	flake	smoke	tune	theme	scrape	spine	choke
sheet	good	cream	paid	float	peach	broil	shout
thirst	herd	shark	spark	spur	bird	cart	born
handle	ramble	ankle	needle	poodle	battle	raffle	fizzle
lotion	picture	motion	mixture	abrasion	intention	emotion	nurture

APPENDIX F

Practice Words for Syllable Division

VCCV SYLLABLE DIVISION PATTERN

VC´V (first choice): Divide between the consonants; accent first syllable.

All closed syllables
basket, bullet, cactus, campus, candid, catnip, classic, coffin, combat, common, conduct, custom, distant, distinct, fabric, format, gallop, gambit, goblin, gospel, happen, helmet, hemlock, insect, insult, kitten, mascot, mitten, napkin, pencil, public, rabbit, rustic, subject, sudden, tonsil, tunnel

Mixed syllables
after, better, bitter, bladder, butter, center, chapter, charter, chimney, cluster, coffee, comfort, comma, corner, costume, curtail, darling, dinner, doctor, donkey, elbow, elder, expert, factor, fancy, fellow, fifty, finger, fortune, furnish, garment, German, glitter, grammar, gutter, hammer, happy, hunger, ladder, luster, market, mellow, member, nectar, parlor, penny, pepper, perfect, plaster, puppy, scarlet, slender, supper, yellow

VC CV´ (second choice): Divide between the consonants; accent the second syllable.

All closed syllables
abduct, affect, collect, command, commit, compel, concrete, conduct, connect, consist, consult, contempt, discuss, enlist, enrich, extinct, inject, insist, intend, pastel, upset

Mixed syllables
absorb, canteen, cartoon, combine, compete, complain, compose, compute, condone, confess, confide, confuse, display, distort, endorse, engage, entire, escape, estate, esteem, invade, perhaps

V´ CCV (third choice): Divide before the first consonant; accent the first syllable.

All open and closed syllables
April, apron, fragrant, macron, secret

VCV SYLLABLE DIVISION PATTERN

V´ CV (first choice): Divide before the consonant; accent the first syllable.

All open and closed syllables
basic, basis, bogus, caper, climax, evil, final, iris, lilac, lotus, nomad, open, raven, robot, silent, sinus, total, totem, tulip, unit, zero

Mixed syllables
baby, decoy, duty, even, favor, fever, fiber, gravy, locate, navy, paper, prelude, rotate, ruby, silent, spider, super, vacate

V´ CV (second choice): Divide before the consonant; accent the second syllable.
All open and closed syllables
beyond, deduct, deflect, depend, depress, divine, lament

(*Note:* In an open, unaccented syllable, *a* is pronounced /ŭ/ as in *parade* and *i* is pronounced /ĭ/ as in *divide.*)

Mixed syllables
crusade, decline, deduce, degree, deny, deport, elope, elude, evoke, promote, result, unite

VC´ V (third choice): Divide after the consonant; accent the first syllable.
cabin, camel, city, civil, clinic, copy, devil, ever, exile, exit, gravel, habit, legend, level, limit, livid, medal, melon, metal, modern, panel, river, robin, salad, second, seven, toxic, travel, value, venom

VCCCV SYLLABLE DIVISION PATTERN

VC´ CCV (first choice): Divide after the first consonant; accent the first syllable.
children, dandruff, escrow, fortress, hamster, hundred, monster, ostrich, pantry, pilgrim, spectrum

VC CCV´ (second choice): Divide after the first consonant; accent the second syllable.
complete, destroy, distract, emblaze, employ, enclose, exclaim, exclude, explain, exploit, extract, extreme, surprise

V´CC CV (third choice): Divide after the second consonant; accent the first syllable.
bankrupt, muskrat, partner, pumpkin, sandwich

V V SYLLABLE DIVISION PATTERN

V´ V (first choice): Divide between the vowels; accent first syllable.
bias, lion, neon, triumph, truant

V´ V (second choice): Divide between the vowels that could but do not form a digraph or a diphthong; accent first syllable.
boa, diet, poem, quiet, stoic

V V´ (third choice): Divide between the vowels; accent the second syllable.
coerce, create, duet

WORDS WITH THREE OR MORE
SYLLABLES TO USE FOR SYLLABLE DIVISION PRACTICE

alfalfa, Atlantic, assemble, basketball, butterfly, carpenter, chinchilla, contradict, controvert, conundrum, cornerstone, counterpart, cucumber, cumulus, dependent, dislocate, elastic, electromagnet, electromotor, encounter, entertain, establish, fantastic, formula, fundamental, gorilla, identify, identity, improvise, independent, insulate, intellect, introduce, investment, justify, membership, nocturnal, particular, peppercorn, peppermint, permeate, porcupine, principle, reinforce, reluctant, republic, resemble, testament, unicorn, vanilla

Suffixes, Prefixes, Roots, and Combining Forms

SUFFIXES

A suffix is a letter or group of letters added to the end of a base word, root, or combining form, to change its form, usage, tense, or meaning.

-able	able to
-al	related to
-ed	past tense
-en	made of
-er	more
-er	one who or that which
-es	more than one
-est	the most
-ful	full of
-ible	able to
-ic	having characteristics of
-ing	happening now
-ish	quality of
-ity	state of
-less	without
-ly	quality of
-ment	state of
-ness	state of
-or	more
-or	one who or that which
-ous	full of
-s	more than one
-y	quality of

PREFIXES

A prefix is a letter or letters added to the beginning of a base word, root, or combining form to change its meaning.

ab-	away from
ad- (ac-, af- ag-, al-, an-, ar-, as-, at-)	to, toward
auto-	self, unaided
be-	to cause, become
bene-	good
bi-	two
circum-	around
con- (co-, com-, cor-)	with, together
contra-	against
counter-	against, in opposition

de-	down, away from
dec-	ten
demi-	half
dis-	the reverse of
dys-	not normal
en- (em-)	to cause, provide
ex-	out of, away from
extra-	outside, beyond
fore-	previously, in front of
hydro-	water
hyper-	extra, beyond, over
hypo-	under, below
in- (il-, im-, ir-)	in, on, toward
in-	not
inter-	between
intra-	inside
micro-	small
mid-	middle
mini-	small
mis-	wrongly, badly
mono-	one, single
non-	not, against
nona-	nine
ob- (oc-, of-, op-)	in the way of
octa-	eight
omni-	all, general
poly-	many
post-	after
pre-	before
pseudo-	false, pretend
quadr-, quar-	four
quint-	five
re-	back, again
retro-	backward
self-	by oneself
semi-	half
sept-	seven
sext-	six
super-	above
trans-	across
tri-	three
ultra-	beyond
un-	not
under-	below, beneath
uni-	one
up-	upper
vice-	in place of

ROOTS (LATIN) AND COMBINING FORMS (GREEK)

aero	Greek air
agri	Latin field
alter	Latin other
ambi	Latin both
ambul	Latin walk
amo	Latin love
andr, anthr	Greek mankind
ang	Latin bend
anim	Latin life, spirit, soul
anni, annu, enni	Latin year
anthropo	Greek human
apt, ept	Latin fasten
aqua	Latin water
arch, archy	Greek ruler, to rule
aristo	Greek best
art	Latin skill
astro	Greek star
atmo	Greek vapor
audi	Latin hear
auto	Greek self
belli	Latin war
biblio	Greek books
bio	Greek life
brev	Latin short
cad, cas, cid	Latin fall or befall
camp	Latin field
capit, capt	Latin head, chief
cardi	Greek heart
caus, cus	Latin cause, motive
cede, ceed, cess	Latin go, yield, surrender
centr	Latin center
cepha	Greek head
cept, cap, ceiv, ceit	Latin seize, take, catch
cern, cert	Latin separate, decide
cess	Latin go, move
chloro	Greek pale green
chromo	Greek color
chrono	Greek time
cide, cise	Latin cut, kill
claim, clam	Latin shout
clar	Latin clear
cogn	Latin know
corp	Latin body
cosmo	Greek universe
crat, cracy	Greek rule
cred	Latin belief
cur, curs, cours	Latin run, go
cycl	Greek circle
demo	Greek people
dent	Latin tooth

derm	Greek	skin
dex	Latin	right
dic, dict	Latin	speak
div	Latin	separate
drome	Greek	run
duc, duce, duct	Latin	lead
dyn, dynamo	Greek	power, force
eco	Greek	house, home
ecto	Greek	outside
ego	Latin	self
endo	Greek	within
eques, equi	Latin	horse
fac, fic, fact, fect	Latin	make
fer	Latin	bring, bear, yield
flect, flex	Latin	bend
form	Latin	shape
gen	Greek	birth
geo	Greek	earth
gon	Greek	angle
grad	Latin	step, degree, walk
graph, gram	Greek	write, record
grat, gre	Latin	pleasing
greg	Latin	gather, group
hal	Latin	breathe
helio	Greek	sun
hema, hemo	Greek	blood
homo	Latin	alike
hydr, hydra	Greek	water
hypn, hypno	Greek	sleep
ideo	Greek	idea
ject	Latin	throw
jud, jur, jus	Latin	law, judge
junct	Latin	join
kin, kine, cine	Greek	move
lat	Latin	side or wide
lect, leg, lig	Latin	choose, read, speak
leg	Latin	law
liber	Latin	free
lith, litho	Greek	stone
loc, loqu	Latin	speak, talk, say
loco	Latin	place
logo, (o)logy	Greek	word, study of
luc, luna, lumin	Latin	light
man, manu	Latin	hand
mania	Greek	madness, obsession
mar	Latin	sea
mech	Greek	machine
memo	Latin	to bring to mind
meter, metr	Greek	measure
mis, mit	Latin	send
mob, mot, mov	Latin	move
mod	Latin	measure

moni	Latin warn
morph, morphe	Greek form
mort	Latin death
myo	Greek muscle
nat	Latin born
naut, naus	Greek sailor, ship
nav	Latin ship
neo	Greek new
nom	Latin name
noun	Latin declare
nov	Latin new
nym	Greek name
ortho	Greek straight, correct
pan, panto	Greek all
path	Greek feeling
ped	Greek child
ped	Latin foot
pel, puls	Latin drive, push
phila, philo	Greek love, affinity for
phobia	Greek irrational fear, hate
phono	Greek sound
photo	Greek light
phyll	Greek leaves
phys	Greek nature
plic, ply	Latin fold
pneumo	Greek breath, lung
pod	Greek foot
pol, poli, polis	Greek city
pon, pos, pose, pound	Latin put, place
pop	Latin people
port	Latin carry
psych	Greek mind
pulmo	Latin lung
pup	Latin child, doll
put, pute	Latin think
ras, raz	Latin scrape
rect	Latin lead straight
rupt	Latin break
san	Latin health
sanct	Latin holy
saur	Greek lizard, serpent
scope	Greek see, watch
scribe, script	Latin write, written
sect	Latin cut
sequi	Latin follow
sist, sta, stat	Latin stand, endure
soph	Greek wisdom, cleverness
spec, spect	Latin see, watch
sphere	Latin circle
spir	Latin breath, breathe
stereo	Greek solid, firm
stru, struct	Latin build

syn, sym	Greek same
tact, tag, tang, tig	Latin touch
techn	Greek art, craft
ten, tend, tain, tin, tinu	Latin have, hold
tend, tens, tent	Latin stretch
theo	Greek God
therm	Greek heat
tort	Latin twist
tract	Latin pull
vac	Latin empty
ven, veni, vent	Latin come
ver, veri	Latin true, genuine
vert, vers	Latin turn
vid, vis	Latin see
vit, vita, viv, vivi	Latin to live
voc, vok, voke	Latin call

Rapid Word-Recognition Chart

Four-Leaf Clover

The four large pieces represent the four checkpoints of the Doubling Rule: one vowel (1V), one consonant (1C), one accent (1′), and a vowel suffix (V in a box). The pieces are placed together to make a four-leaf clover. If all checkpoints are present, the fifth piece (the stem) is added, signifying that the final consonant of the base word or root is doubled. See Try This H for directions on how to make the four-leaf clover.

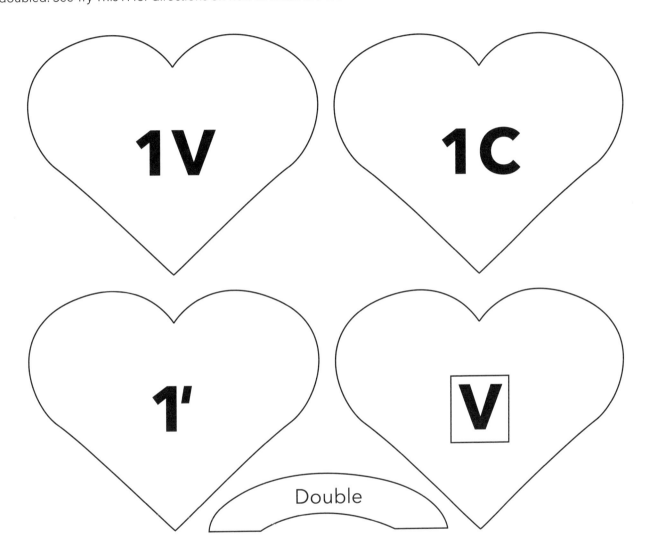

Word Webs

Semantic Web

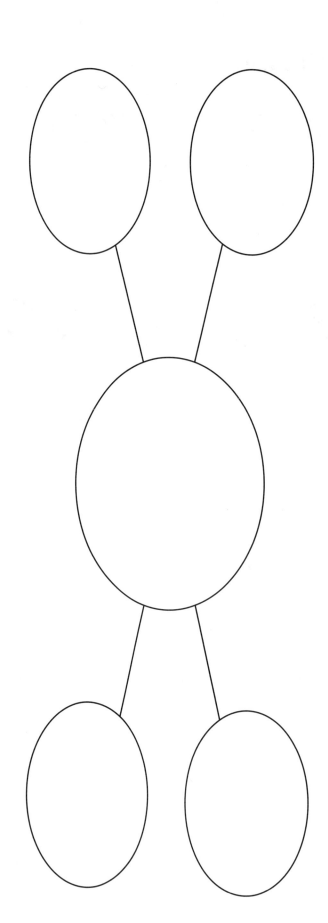

Multisensory Teaching of Basic Language Skills Activity Book, Fourth Edition, by Suzanne Carreker and Judith R. Birsh

Derivative or Multiple Meaning Web

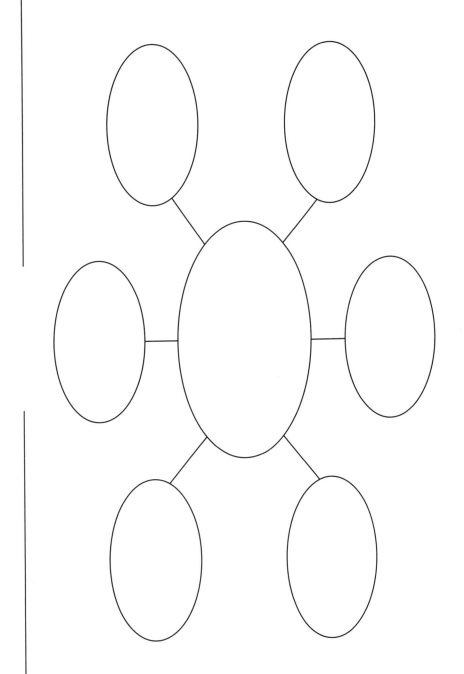

Multisensory Teaching of Basic Language Skills Activity Book, Fourth Edition, by Suzanne Carreker and Judith R. Birsh.
Copyright © 2019 by Paul H. Brookes Publishing Co., Inc. All rights reserved.

Semantic Feature Analysis

Key: √ = a relationship; X = a nonrelationship; ? = unsure of a relationship.

Word Profile

Word:_____

Number of phonemes: _____   Phonemes: _____

Rime pattern: _____

Number of letters: _____   Letters: _____

Number of graphemes: _____   Graphemes: _____

Spelling pattern (Is there a regular pattern or rule, or is the word irregular?):

_____

_____

Origin: _____

Derivatives: _____

_____

One definition: _____

_____

_____

Multiple meanings: _____

_____

_____

Synonyms: _____

_____

Antonyms: _____

_____

Part(s) of speech: _____

Usage (formal or informal): _____

Figurative usages: _____

_____

Comprehension Passages

Rhinoceroses

Rhinoceroses are among the largest of land animals. The word *rhinoceros* comes from the Greek words *rhinos* (nose) and *keratos* (horn). The rhinoceros or rhino is distinguishable by its horned nose. Sadly, its horn has made it a critically endangered animal. People hunt and kill them and sell their horns on the black market for a lot of money. The horns are used to make jewelry and medicine. Some people collect the horns as trophies. As a result of the buying and selling, rhinoceroses may totally disappear on Earth.

There are five different species, or kinds, of rhinoceroses: Black, White, Sumatran, Javan, and Indian. The white rhino is almost entirely extinct. Only five white rhinos remain in captivity in zoos. When these five rhinos die, this species will no longer exist.

Rhinoceroses can weigh anywhere between 1,700 to 7,000 pounds. They are herbivores. That means they eat only plants. Some species of rhinoceros eat mostly grasses. Other species prefer to eat leaves from bushes and trees. If they avoid capture, they can live up to 35 years.

Dollars to Donuts or Is It Doughnuts?

Do you know what Americans celebrate on the first Friday of June every year? And have been celebrating since 1938? It's National Doughnut Day or National Donut Day! So, why are there two different spellings of this popular sweet treat?

The traditional spelling is *doughnut*. This spelling actually describes the original form of the treat. That is, dough was rolled into a ball and deep fried in hot fat. When fried, the balls resembled walnuts or chestnuts. No one knows the true story of how the ring shape became the most familiar shape for doughnuts.

The other spelling of the word is pure marketing. The spelling *donut* was thought to be easier for people to read—no silent letters. Although the spelling *donut* is the favorite in the United States, the preferred spelling everywhere else is *doughnut*.

The phrase *dollars to donuts* is an American phrase that suggests dollars are more valuable than donuts. So, betting your dollars to someone else's donuts is a safe bet. I bet you dollars to donuts that you didn't know that Americans eat more than 5 billion dollars' worth of donuts each year. That's a lot of dough!

The Rabbit, the Weasel, and the Dog

One day a rabbit left his house to gather some green plants for his dinner. As he left, he forgot to close and lock the door. While he was gone, a rather bold weasel discovered the unlocked door and calmly made himself at home—permanently.

When the rabbit returned, he was upset to see that the weasel had made himself at home. When he learned that the weasel did not intend to leave, he was even more upset. The rabbit and the weasel began to argue loudly. Their arguing woke a wise old dog from her nap. She needed to settle the argument to stop the noise.

"I am very deaf," she said, "You will need to come close to my ears. One of you by each ear. Then tell me all the facts."

The unsuspecting pair did as the dog requested. In an instant, the dog had both of them under her paws. The argument was soon settled. The weasel found a new home, the rabbit was satisfied, and the wise old dog, who was not so deaf after all, enjoyed peace and quiet.

Sometimes a third party is helpful in resolving a conflict.

✳

Georgianna and the Lemonade Stand

Georgianna loved wearing the latest fashions. The only problem was that she never had any money to buy them.

"Only 10 dollars and 9 cents," she said disappointedly after she emptied her piggy bank. "That won't buy me much. How can I make some money to buy new clothes?"

Georgianna made a list of things she could do to make money. Most of them would take too long or were too much work. The one thing she thought was perfect was opening a lemonade stand. It was summertime. Lemonade is refreshing. There were a lot of people in her neighborhood.

She would need to spend some of her money to buy lemonade mix, paper cups, and ice. So, she figured out the costs and the possible income. "An investment of 8 dollars will bring me as much as 32 dollars a day if I sell each cup of lemonade for 50 cents," she calculated. "And if I do this for 5 days, that'll buy me plenty of new clothes!"

As Georgianna walked to the store to buy the lemonade mix, paper cups, and ice, she thought about her new clothes. When she got home, she mixed up the lemonade. She set up her stand on the sidewalk outside her apartment building. She had two of her mother's 2-gallon glass jugs full of lemonade, the paper cups, and a large bucket of ice. As she waited for customers, she continued to dream of all the new clothes that would hang in her closet. The first potential customers scoffed at the cost of the lemonade and passed on by. So, she lowered the price to 45 cents a cup.

As the day went on, there were still no sales. No matter, Georgianna pictured each new outfit she would wear when school started in the fall. She didn't notice that the sun was melting her ice. Or, that a gust of wind had blown most of her cups into the trash-filled gutter. And then, an unleashed Great Dane smashed right into her stand and knocked it over. Down went the jugs in a crash and a splash! When everything was cleaned up, Georgiana had only 2 dollars and 9 cents left in her piggy bank.

What might be the moral of this story?

Types of Math Deficits

PROCEDURAL DEFICITS
Operational dyscalculia (Geary, 2004)
Procedural (Kosc, 1974)

Difficulties with
Procedures in (written) calculation
Sequencing multiple steps in complex procedures
Planning or execution of complex operations
Mental calculations
Routines

As well as
Immature strategies
Many mistakes with complex procedures
Time-lag in arithmetic procedures
Poor understanding of concepts in procedures

SEMANTIC MEMORY DEFICITS
R-S profile (Rourke & Conway, 1997)
Semantic memory deficits (Geary, 2004)

Difficulties with
Acquisition of number facts
Retrieval of numerical facts
Semantic-acoustic aspect of linguistic domain
Conceptual knowledge terms
Language comprehension
Passive vocabulary
Orally presented terms

As well as
Low accuracy in mental calculation
Slow speed of mental and written calculation
Irregular reaction times
High error rate
Wrong associations in retrieval
Low enumerating speed for figures, symbols, numbers, and quantities

---

VISUOSPATIAL DEFICITS
Practognostic dyscalculia (Kosc, 1974)
Nonverbal learning disorder (Rourke & Conway, 1997)
Visualspatial subtype (Geary, 2004)

Difficulties with
Placing numbers on a number line
Understanding geometry
Abstraction
Temporal order or planning
Novel and complex tasks
Symbol recognition
Insight in and notions of space

Disturbance in
Setting out objects in order according to magnitude
Visuospatial memory
Visual imaginative faculty
Enumerating groups of objects
Estimating and comparing quantities

Difficulties with
Inversions and reversals in numbers
Misinterpretation of spatially represented information
Visual neglect

As well as
Misalignment and misplacements of digits
Nonverbal impairments
Eventually dyspraxia

NUMBER KNOWLEDGE DEFICITS
Verbal-Lexical-Graphical-Ideognostic dyscalculia (Kosc, 1974)
Arabic dyscalculia, Pervasive dyscalculia (von Aster, 2000)

Difficulties with
Understanding Arabic notation, math ideas, and relations
Abstract number comprehension
Transcoding between the different modalities
In size comparison
Number ordering
Enumeration
Number dictation

Disturbance in
Number knowledge
Basic sense of numerosity
Encoding the semantics of numbers
Number reading
Number writing
Number production

Figure N.1. Adapted from the Dyscalculia Classification Chart, Stock, Desoete, and Roeyers (2006). (From Garnett, K., & Uscianowski, C. [2018]. Math learning disabilities. In J.R. Birsh & S. Carreker [Eds.], *Multisensory teaching of basic language skills* (4th ed., p. 515). Baltimore, MD: Paul H. Brookes Publishing Co.; reprinted by permission.)

Building Block Checklist for Effective Classroom Management

Directions:

1. Read through all items in the Building Block Checklist.

2. In the left column, place a check mark next to each item currently being addressed.

3. In the right column, place a check mark next to each item that needs to change to improve classroom management.

Things I am doing	Aspect of planning	Things I want to do differently
	Classroom environment	
	Bulletin boards	
	Furniture	
	Student desks	
	Traffic pattern(s)	
	Teacher organization	
	Teacher(s) desk(s)	
	Organization of teaching materials	
	Plan for instructional transitions	
	Student behavior	
	Establishment of classroom rules and expectations	
	Reduction of student anxiety	
	Bonding and connecting with all students	
	Connecting with individual students	
	Active listening to students	

	Self-evaluation of classroom needs	
	Is it a safe environment?	
	Can students take academic risks?	
	Are students exploring friendships?	
	Are students negotiating the classroom setting?	
	Are students learning appropriate expectations and behaviors?	
	Are students' behaviors transferable to the outside world?	

Multisensory Teaching of Basic Language Skills Activity Book, Fourth Edition, by Suzanne Carreker and Judith R. Birsh.

Answer Key

ACTIVITY 1–TERMS FOR RESEARCH AND STRUCTURED LITERACY

1) r, 2) q, 3) p, 4) k, 5) m, 6) l, 7) a, 8) d, 9) g, 10) n, 11) h, 12) e, 13) b, 14) i, 15) f, 16) c, 17) j, 18) o

ACTIVITY 2–THE BRAIN

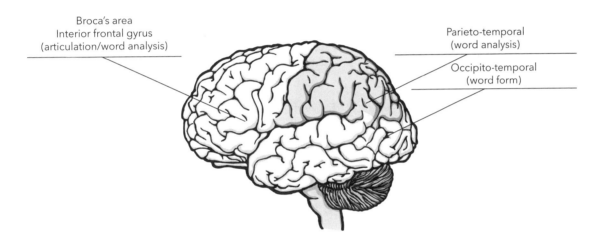

Broca's area
Interior frontal gyrus
(articulation/word analysis)

Parieto-temporal
(word analysis)

Occipito-temporal
(word form)

From Kaufman, C. (2011). *Executive function in the classroom: Practical strategies for improving performance and enhancing skills for all students* (p. 27). Baltimore, MD: Paul H. Brookes Publishing Co.; reprinted by permission.

ACTIVITY 3–STRUCTURED LITERACY TERMS

1) d, 2) c, 3) g, 4) f, 5) b, 6) a, 7) h, 8) e, 9) l, 10) j, 11) m, 12) i, 13) n, 14) k

ACTIVITY 4–TERMS FOR ORAL LANGUAGE

1) f, 2) e, 3) b, 4) g, 5) h, 6) a, 7) j, 8) i, 9) c, 10) d

ACTIVITY 5–PHONEMES: VOWELS

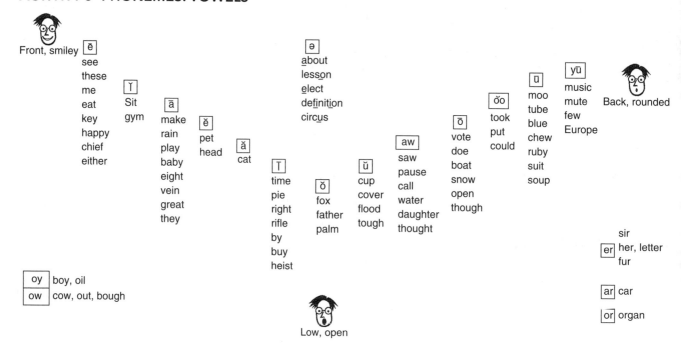

From Moats, LC. (2010). *Speech to print: Language essentials for teachers* (2nd ed., p. 96). Baltimore, MD: Paul H. Brookes Publishing Co.; adapted by permission.

ACTIVITY 6–WHAT CHILDREN KNOW AND WHAT THEY CAN EXPLORE

Answers will vary.

ACTIVITY 7–OPEN-ENDED QUESTIONS

Answers will vary.

ACTIVITY 8–LETTER SHAPES AND NAMES

All straight lines	All curved lines	Straight and curved lines
A, E, F, H, I K, L, M, N, T, V, W, X, Y, Z, i, k, l, t, v, w, x, y, z	C, O, S, U, c, o, s	B, D, G, J, P, Q, R, a, b, d, e, f, g, h, j, m, n, p, q, r, u

ACTIVITY 9–PHONEMIC AWARENESS ACTIVITIES

Isolation/identification: 4, 6, 8, 11

Blending: 1, 12

Segmentation: 3, 7, 10

Deletion/addition: 2, 5, 9

ACTIVITY 10–HOW MANY PHONEMES?

mat (3), cash (3), ship (3), match (3), stop (4), knife (3), scratch (5), truck, (4), love (3), spell (4), stand (5), child (4), month (4), think (4), peach (3), queen (4), train (4), climb (4), strike (5), blank (5)

ACTIVITY 11–HOW MANY PHONEMES?

show (2), splint (6), knee (2), badge (3), past (4), face (3), thrill (4), clock (4), give (3), shack (3), strand (6), teeth (3), church (3), shrink (5), enough (4), quit (4), fix (4), smile (4), night (3), flax (5)

ACTIVITY 12–SAME PHONEME?

(yes = the phonemes are the same; no = the phonemes are different)

said/bed (yes); spins/spins (no); bath/safe (no); steak/vein (yes); night/tie (yes); market/mustard (no); that/vase (no); peach/priest (yes); plaid/blast (yes); orbit/actor (no); arch/echo (no); splint/jumped (yes); sink/sing (yes); first/fern (yes); tense/face (yes); fly/penny (no); rhythm/rhyme (no); zipper/pansy (yes); graft/graph (yes); landed/seemed (no)

ACTIVITY 13–SAME PHONEME?

(yes = the phonemes are the same; no = the phonemes are different)

view/shoe (yes); wash/mash (no); tent/tent (yes); boy/boil (yes); canyon/yellow (yes); doctor/shortage (no); shack/wash (yes); isle/spy (yes); room/fruit (yes); ballet/survey (yes); that/with (no); single/finger (yes); jeep/girl (no); raw/haul (yes); gem/jet (yes); water/polish (yes or no depending regional pronunciation); heal/health (no); group/grout (no); troop/soup (yes); gas/his (no)

ACTIVITY 14–HOW MANY LETTERS AND HOW MANY PHONEMES?

broom (5, 4); knee (4, 2); shrimp (6, 5); splint (6, 6); sprint (6, 6); lead (4, 3); grasp (5, 5); sound (5, 4); blame (5, 4); sing (4, 3); mix (3, 4); show (4, 2); left (4, 4); child (5, 4); space (5, 4); teach (5, 3); both (4, 3); spend (5, 5); kind (4, 4); knowledge (9, 5)

ACTIVITY 15–HOW MANY LETTERS AND HOW MANY PHONEMES?

judge (5, 3); need (4, 3); peach (5, 3); thrill (6, 4); know (4, 2); plan (4, 4); clasp (5, 5); knife (5, 3); may (3, 2); stray (5, 4); most (4, 4); shout (5, 3); shrill (6, 4); less (4, 3); close (5, 4); cloth (5, 4); splice (6, 5); trend (5, 5); jacket (6, 5); muskrat (7, 7)

ACTIVITY 16–PHONEMES: VOICED AND UNVOICED CONSONANTS

Voiced: /b/, /d/, /g/, /j/, /l/, /m/, /n/, /ng/, /r/, /th/, /v/, /w/, /y/, /z/, /zh/
Unvoiced: /ch/, /f/, /h/, /hw/, /k/, /p/, /s/, /sh/, /t/, /th/

ACTIVITY 17–PHONEME CHECKLIST

/l/ as in *leaf* (blocked, voiced, continuant)
/d/ as in *dog* (partially blocked, voiced, clipped)
/g/ as in *goat* (partially blocked, voiced, clipped)
/b/ as in *bat* (partially blocked, voiced, clipped)
/th/ as in *thin* (blocked, unvoiced, continuant)

/ch/ as in *chin* (partially blocked, unvoiced, clipped)

/w/ as in *wagon* (blocked, voiced, continuant)

/h/ as in *house* (open, unvoiced; /h/ is the only consonant sound that opens the mouth; all other consonant sounds are blocked or partially blocked)

/m/ as in *mitten* (blocked, voiced, continuant)

/j/ as in *jump* (partially blocked, voiced, clipped)

/zh/ as in *erosion* (blocked, voiced, continuant)

/s/ as in *sock* (blocked, unvoiced, continuant)

ACTIVITY 18–PHONEME CHECKLIST

/y/ as in *yellow* (partially blocked, voiced, clipped)

/z/ as in *zipper* (blocked, voiced, continuant)

/n/ as in *nest* (blocked, voiced, continuant)

/ng/ as in *sink* (blocked, voiced, continuant)

/k/ as in *kite* (partially blocked, unvoiced, clipped)

/p/ as in *pig* (partially blocked, unvoiced, clipped)

/sh/ as in *ship* (blocked, unvoiced, continuant)

/t/ as in *table* (partially blocked, unvoiced, clipped)

/f/ as in *fish* (blocked, unvoiced, continuant)

/th/ as in *mother* (blocked, voiced, continuant)

/v/ as in *valentine* (blocked, voiced, continuant)

/r/ as in *rabbit* (blocked, voiced, continuant)

ACTIVITY 19–CLASSIFICATION OF PHONEMES

1) b, 2) e, 3) c, 4) a, 5) f, 6) d, 7) i, 8) g, 9) j, 10) h, 11) l, 12) k

ACTIVITY 20 –TERMS FOR ASSESSMENT

1) n, 2) e, 3) k, 4) d, 5) b, 6) m, 7) l, 8) g, 9) o, 10) f, 11) j, 12) i, 13) a, 14) c, 15) h

ACTIVITY 21–EXECUTIVE FUNCTION: LANGUAGE

Answers will vary.

ACTIVITY 22–EXECUTIVE FUNCTION: WORKING MEMORY

Answers will vary.

ACTIVITY 23–EXECUTIVE FUNCTION: MAKING CONNECTIONS

Answers will vary.

ACTIVITY 24–EXECUTIVE FUNCTION: METACOGNITION AND SELF-REGULATION

Answers will vary.

ACTIVITY 25–READING PATTERNS

c is pronounced /k/ before *a, o, u,* or any consonant. (*cat, cup, cot, clasp, crib*)

c is pronounced /s/ before *e, i,* or *y.* (*cycle, city, cent*)

g is pronounced /g/ before *a, o, u,* or any consonant. (*gate, got, gum, glad*)

g is pronounced /j/ before *e, i,* or *y.* (*gem, gist, gypsy, gym*)

n is pronounced /n/ in initial, final, or medial position. (*nap, snip, spin*)

n is pronounced /ng/ before any letter that is pronounced /k/ or /g/. (*sink, sanctuary, vanquish, finger, angle*)

x is pronounced /ks/ in medial or final position. (*expel, exit, box, relax*)

x is pronounced /z/ in initial position. (*xylophone, xenophobia, xylem*)

y is pronounced /y/ in initial position. (*yank, yield, Yule, yellow, yogurt*)

y is pronounced /ī/ at the end of an accented syllable. (*supply, reply, shy, fly*)

y is pronounced /ē/ at the end of a word in unaccented syllable. (*empty, penny, happy*)

ACTIVITY 26–HARD AND SOFT c AND g

city (soft before i), *gem* (soft before e), *clown* (hard before a consonant), *cent* (soft before e), *fancy* (soft before y), *gym* (soft before y), *gist* (soft before i), *space* (soft before e), *energy* (soft before y), *inclusion* (hard before a consonant), *exigent* (soft before e), *facility* (soft before i), *gentleman* (soft before e), *bicycle* (soft before y), *bicycle* (hard before a consonant), *difficult* (hard before u), *registration* (soft before i), *faculty* (hard before u)

ACTIVITY 27–LETTER CLUSTERS

bl (blend), *sh* (digraph), *mp* (blend), *th* (digraph), *nk* (blend), *nt* (blend), *ck* (digraph), *wh* (digraph), *ch* (digraph), *dr* (blend)

The vowel pairs *ea, oe, oo, oa, ai, au,* and *aw* are digraphs; *oi, oy, ou,* and *ow* are diphthongs. (*Note:* The vowel pair *ou* as in *soup* is considered a digraph; however, it is infrequently used.)

ACTIVITY 28–HOW MANY LETTERS AND HOW MANY GRAPHEMES?

bridge (6, 4); wheel (5, 3); church (6, 3); school (6, 4); show (4, 2); band (4, 4); feet (4, 3); knife (5, 3); phone (5, 3); song (4, 3); breath (6, 4); slant (5, 5); stack (5, 4); shack (5, 3); sketch (6, 4); hand (4, 4); finish (6, 5); straw (5, 4); head (4, 3); shroud (6, 4)

ACTIVITY 29–HOW MANY LETTERS AND HOW MANY GRAPHEMES?

deck (4, 3); lamp (4, 4); bench (5, 4); smoke (5, 4); glow (4, 3); shrine (6, 4); cheese (6, 3); pencil (6, 6); state (5, 4); strong (6, 5); teacher (7, 4); phone (5, 3); sports (6, 5); plate (5, 4); stretch (7, 5); strand (6, 6); clover (6, 5); start (5, 4); seed (4, 3); threat (6, 4)

ACTIVITY 30–VOWEL PAIRS

The first vowel does the talking: *ai* (paint), *ay* (play), *ea* (teach), *ee* (feet), *ei* (ceiling), *ey* (monkey), *ie* (tie), *oa* (boat), *oe* (toe), *ow* (show), *ue* (statue)

The first vowel does not do the talking: *au* (saucer), *aw* (saw), *ea* (head), *ea* (steak), *ei* (vein), *eu* (Europe), *ew* (pew), *ie* (priest), *oi* (oil), *oo* (book), *oo* (moon), *ou* (out), *ow* (cow), *oy* (boy), *ui* (fruit)

ACTIVITY 31—VOWEL-*r* PATTERNS

/er/: *ar* (dollar), *er* (fern), *er* (letter), *ir* (first), *ir* (tapir), *or* (doctor), *or* (work), *ur* (fur), *ur* (murmur)

/ar/: *ar* (star)

/or/: *ar* (warm), *ar* (quart), *or* (fork)

The patterns *er, ir,* and *ur* are always pronounced /er/.

In an accented syllable, *ar* is pronounced /ar/ and *or* is pronounced /or/.

In an unaccented syllable, *ar* and *or* are pronounced /er/.

After /w/, *or* is pronounced /er/.

After /w/, *ar* is pronounced /or/.

ACTIVITY 32—SYLLABLE TYPE DEFINITIONS

1) d, 2) e, 3) f, 4) c, 5) a, 6) b

ACTIVITY 33—SORTING SYLLABLE TYPES: CLOSED, OPEN, VOWEL-*r*

Open: *so, he, me, we*

Closed: *hiss, sod, hen, hem, met, west, fond, hand, spun, cat, fist*

Vowel-r: *firm, car, spur, fork, hard*

ACTIVITY 34—SORTING SYLLABLE TYPES: CLOSED, OPEN, VOWEL PAIRS

Closed: *miss, help, bond, stomp, send*

Vowel pairs: *seed, toast, book, heap, maid, free, deep, mood, beet, play*

Open: *so, fly, be, cry, me*

ACTIVITY 35—SORTING SYLLABLE TYPES

Closed: *not, hen, mettle, men, hit, lost, shamble, pick, picture, went*

Open: *no, noble, he, me, hi, locate, she, supreme, so, we, my*

Vowel-consonant-e: *note, here, hive, lone, lore, locate, shine, supreme, mine*

Vowel-r: *nor, her, short, portion, work, warm, marble*

Vowel pair: *noon, heat, meet, mean, loan, low, sheep, pie, peek, soak, weep*

Final stable or consonant-*le*: *noble, mettle, picture, portion, marble, shamble*

ACTIVITY 36—WHICH SYLLABLE TYPE?

lump (closed), *smoke* (vowel-consonant-e), *she* (open), *speech* (vowel pair), *clutch* (closed), *strict* (closed), *thirst* (vowel-r), *porch* (vowel-r), *stray* (vowel pair), *bottle* (final stable or consonant-*le*), *monster* (vowel-r), *moisture* (vowel pair), *simple* (final stable or consonant-*le*), *hundred* (closed), *solo* (open), *perfect* (vowel-r), *extreme* (vowel-consonant-e), *publish* (closed), *circle* (final stable or consonant-*le*), *frequent* (open)

ACTIVITY 37—GENERATING SYLLABLE TYPES

Answers will vary.

ACTIVITY 38—SYLLABLE DIVISION PATTERNS

mascot (VCCV), rotate (VCV), monster (VCCCV), bias (V V), tactic (VCCV), cabin (VCV), lion (V V), supreme (VCCV), portray (VCCCV), second (VCV), pumpkin (VCCCV), truant (V V), surround (VCCV), instant (VCCCV), item (VCV), convoy (VCCV), instinct (VCCCV), report (VCV), contrast (VCCCV), connect (VCCV)

ACTIVITY 39—WHERE TO DIVIDE VCCV AND VCV WORDS?

chip munk, lo tus, dis tance, pig ment, en tice, ban ner, du ty, de tain, es cape, ba by, par ty, pro vide, lo cal, stub born, be low, mar ket, lo cate, cop per, re late, rib bon

ACTIVITY 40—WHERE TO DIVIDE VCCCV AND V V WORDS?

cha os, li on, dis trict, po em, ex treme, con struct, du et, des troy, pump kin, musk rat, part ner, ru in, du al, dis tract, bi as, con tract, da is, tru ant, mis spell, spec trum

ACTIVITY 41—ACCENT

spi' der, **bo'** a, pre **dict'**, **con'** stant, con **trol'**, **na'** vy, **qui'** et, pas **tel'**, **en'** ter, can **teen'**, **sev'** en, be **cause'**, **cham'** ber, **con'** voy, **tri'** al, **spec'** trum, **pump'** kin, **tri'** umph, de **cide'**, **chal'** lenge

ACTIVITY 42—SYLLABLE DIVISION PATTERNS AND CHOICES

mascot (VCCV, first); rotate (VCV, first); monster (VCCCV, first); bias (V V, first); tactic (VCCV, first); cabin (VCV, third); lion (V V, first); supreme (VCCV, second); portray (VCCCV, second); second (VCV, third); pumpkin (VCCCV, third); truant (V V, first); surround (VCCV, second); instant (VCCCV, first); item (VCV, first); convoy (VCCV, first); instinct (VCCCV, first); report (VCV, second); contrast (VCCCV, first and second); connect (VCCV, second)

ACTIVITY 43—SHORT VOWELS IN VOWEL-*r* SYLLABLES

merry (/ĕ/), corner (/or/, /er/), first (/er/), carry (/â/), very (/ĕ/), survey (/er/), cherry (/ĕ/), errand (/ĕ/), garlic (/ar/), derrick (/ĕ/), ferret (/ĕ/), sherbet (/er/), merit (/ĕ/), barrack (/â/), harness (/ar/), error (/ĕ/), orbit (/or/), carrot (/â/), urgent (/er/), narrow (/â/)

ACTIVITY 44—TERMS FOR DECODING

1) j, 2) b, 3) e, 4) i, 5) k, 6) d, 7) m, 8) f, 9) n, 10) h, 11) a, 12) p, 13) g, 14) o, 15) c, 16) l

ACTIVITY 45—VOWEL AND CONSONANT SUFFIXES

Vowel suffixes: *-en, -ity, -ous, -able, -ish, -ist*
Consonant suffixes: *-ment, -ful, -ness, -less, -ly, -ward*

ACTIVITY 46—INFLECTIONAL ENDING *-s*

seems /z/, jumps /s/, lands /z/, starts /s/, lists /s/, picks /s/, likes /s/, settles /z/, copes /s/, spells /z/, camps /s/, distributes /s/, recycles /z/, screams /z/, grasps /s/

ACTIVITY 47—INFLECTIONAL ENDING *-ed*

seemed (/d/), jumped (/t/), landed (/ĕd/), started (/ĕd/), tossed (/t/), picked (/t/), listed (/ĕd/), settled (/d/), copied (/d/), spelled (/d/), camped (/t/), distributed (/ĕd/), recycled (/d/), enclosed (/d/), realized (/d/)

ACTIVITY 48–INFLECTIONAL AND DERIVATIONAL SUFFIXES

Base word	Part of speech	Derivative	Part of speech	Ending or suffix	Inflectional	Derivational
desk	noun	desks	noun	-s	✓	
help	noun or verb	helpless	adjective	-less		✓
big	adjective	bigger	adjective	-er	✓	
mow	noun or verb	mowing	noun or verb	-ing	✓	
play	noun or verb	playful	adjective	-ful		✓
sky	noun	skies	noun	-es	✓	
love	noun or verb	lovely	adjective	-ly		✓
small	adjective	smallest	adjective	-est	✓	
gentle	adjective	gentleness	noun	-ness		✓
slow	adjective	slower	adjective	-er	✓	
merry	adjective	merriment	noun	-ment		✓

ACTIVITY 49–IRREGULAR WORDS FOR READING

shoe, country, busy, ghost, lamb, said, does, doubt, four, ocean, enough, aisle, friend, plaid, from, would, two, colonel

ACTIVITY 50–REGULAR OR IRREGULAR FOR READING?

done (I), down (R), one (I), tone (R), again (I), paint (R), seed (R), seat (R), came (R), come (I), lose (I), lone (R), back (R), buy (I), pretty (I), plenty (R), become (I), began (R), any (I), orange (I)

ACTIVITY 51–REGULAR OR IRREGULAR FOR READING?

couch (R), some (I), whose (I), could (I), sole (R), soul (I), eye (I), many (I), trust (R), truth (I), debt (I), dead (R), people (I), queen (R), between (R), together (I), trouble (I), tremble (R), woman (I), were (I), should (I), where (I), why (R), match (R)

ACTIVITY 52–CONSONANT PHONEMES: PLACE OF ARTICULATION

Both lips: /b/, /m/, /p/, /w/
Teeth and lower lip: /f/, /v/
Between the teeth: /th/, /th/
Ridge behind the teeth: /d/, /l/, /n/, /r/, /s/, /t/, /z/
Roof of the mouth: /ch/, /j/, /sh/, /y/, /zh/
Back of the mouth: /g/, /k/, /ng/
From the throat: /h/

ACTIVITY 53–CONSONANT PHONEMES: BLOCKED, PARTIALLY BLOCKED, AND UNBLOCKED

Blocked: /f/, /l/, /m/, /n/, /ng/, /r/, /s/, /sh/, /th/, /<u>th</u>/, /v/, /w/, /z/, /zh/

Partially blocked: /b/, /ch/, /d/, /g/, /j/, /k/, /p/, /t/, /y/

Unblocked: /h/

ACTIVITY 54–CONSONANT PHONEMES: CONTINUANT AND CLIPPED

/t/ (clipped), /m/ (continuant), /p/ (clipped), /n/ (continuant), /s/ (continuant), /l/ (continuant), /j/ (clipped), /b/ (clipped), /g/ (clipped), /v/ (continuant), /y/ (clipped), /r/ (continuant), /z/ (continuant), /d/ (clipped)

ACTIVITY 55–CONSONANT PHONEMES: COGNATES

Cognates: /ch/ and /j/, /t/ and /d/, /f/ and /v/, /k/ and /g/, /p/ and /b/, /s/ and /z/, /sh/ and /zh/, /th/ and /<u>th</u>/

ACTIVITY 56–PARTIAL OR COMPLETE PHONETIC REPRESENTATION FOR SPELLING

st for *seat* (partial), *kat* for *cat* (complete), *ct* for *seat* (complete), *gv* for *give* (partial), *whl* for *while* (partial), *jumpt* for *jumped* (complete), *rede* for *read* (complete), *yl* for *while* (complete), *sop* for *soap* (complete), *plez* for *please* (complete), *sep* for *step* (partial), *pik* for *pick* (complete), *mn* for *man* (partial), *moshun* for *motion* (complete), *teme* for *team* (complete), *cutry* for *country* (partial), *hav* for *have* (complete), *samd* for *seemed* (partial), *batel* for *battle* (complete), *enuf* for *enough* (complete), *lafent* for *elephant* (complete), *selebr8* for *celebrate* (complete), *site* for *city* (complete), *split* for *splint* (partial), *sd* for *said* (partial), *wun* for *one* (complete)

ACTIVITY 57–IDENTIFYING SPELLING PATTERNS

empl<u>oy</u>, /oi/, final /oi/ is spelled *oy*

gr<u>ou</u>nd, /ou/, medial /ou/ is spelled *ou*

<u>g</u>iant, /j/, /j/ before *i* is spelled *g*

gr<u>ee</u>n, /ē/, medial /ē/ in a one-syllable word is spelled *ee*

ma<u>tch</u>, /ch/, final /ch/ after a short vowel in a one-syllable word is spelled *tch*

tun<u>a</u>, /ŭ/, final /ŭ/ is spelled *a*

p<u>o</u>lite, /ō/, /ō/ at the end of a syllable is spelled *o*

<u>c</u>andy, /k/, /k/ before *a* is spelled *c*

lila<u>c</u>, /k/, final /k/ after a short vowel in a multisyllabic word is spelled *c*

ugl<u>y</u>, /ē/, final /ē/ at the end of a word with two or more syllables is spelled *y*

por<u>ch</u>, /ch/, final /ch/ after a consonant is spelled *ch*

sh<u>y</u>, /ī/, final /ī/ is spelled *y*

w<u>a</u>sp, /ŏ/, /ŏ/ after *w* is spelled *a*

blo<u>ck</u>, /k/, final /k/ after a short vowel in a one-syllable word is spelled *ck*

dod<u>ge</u>, /j/, final /j/ after a short vowel in a one-syllable word is spelled *dge*

<u>sk</u>ill, /k/, /k/ before *i* is spelled *k*

tr<u>ay</u>, /ā/, /ā/ in final position is spelled *ay*

fl<u>ee</u>, /ē/, final /ē/ in a one-syllable word is spelled *ee*

ACTIVITY 58—FIVE SPELLING RULES

1) b, 2) c, 3) a, 4) e, 5) d

ACTIVITY 59—RULE WORDS

hills (hill + s; the Floss Rule)
letters (letter + s; the Rabbit Rule)
swimmer (swim + er; the Doubling Rule)
happiness (happy + ness; the Changing Rule)
racer (race + er; the Dropping Rule)
dresses (dress + es; the Floss Rule)
reddish (red + ish; the Doubling Rule)
beginning (begin + ing; the Doubling Rule)
penniless (penny + less; the Changing Rule)
muffins (muffin + s; the Rabbit Rule)
engaging (engage + ing; the Dropping Rule)
omitted (omit + ed; the Doubling Rule)
plentiful (plenty + ful; the Changing Rule)
enticing (entice + ing; the Dropping Rule)
settled (settle + ed; the Dropping Rule)
emptied (empty + ed; the Changing Rule)
preferred (prefer + ed; the Doubling Rule)
permitted (permit + ed; the Doubling Rule)

ACTIVITY 60—CHECKPOINTS FOR THE DOUBLING RULE

	One vowel	One consonant	One accent	Vowel suffix	Derivative
hot + est	✓	✓	✓	✓	hottest
run + er	✓	✓	✓	✓	runner
star + ing	✓	✓	✓	✓	starring
cup + ful	✓	✓	✓		cupful
steep + est		✓	✓	✓	steepest
stand + ing	✓		✓	✓	standing
camp + er	✓		✓	✓	camper
child + ish	✓		✓	✓	childish
art + ist	✓		✓	✓	artist
open + er	✓	✓		✓	opener
begin + er	✓	✓	✓	✓	beginner

	One vowel	One consonant	One accent	Vowel suffix	Derivative
benefit + ed	✓	✓		✓	benefited[a]
omit + ed	✓	✓	✓	✓	omitted
travel + ing	✓	✓		✓	traveling[a]
forget + able	✓	✓	✓	✓	forgettable

[a]The preferred spelling of these words in the United States is without the doubled final consonant in the base word, which matches the Doubling Rule. In the United Kingdom, the doubled final consonant in the base word is preferred.

ACTIVITY 61—ANALYZING WORDS FOR SPELLING

Regular	**Rule**	**Irregular (the irregular part is underlined)**
pitch	batting	gl<u>o</u>ve
homerun	runner	<u>one</u>
three	slider	<u>no</u>thing
shortstop		s<u>ea</u>son
player		
manager		
strike		
foul		

ACTIVITY 62—REGULAR, RULE, OR IRREGULAR FOR SPELLING

Regular	**Rule**	**Irregular (the irregular part is underlined)**
banana	cherry	ras<u>p</u>berry
lime	strawberry	or<u>ange</u>
grape	apple	k<u>iwi</u>
coconut	pineapple	p<u>ea</u>r
sand	swimmer	<u>o</u>cean
water	sunning	life<u>g</u>uard
starfish	jellyfish	<u>s</u>wordfish
waves	diving	s<u>ea</u>weed

ACTIVITY 63—REGULAR OR IRREGULAR FOR READING AND SPELLING?

spend (regular for reading and spelling)

said (irregular for reading—the word should be pronounced /sād/; irregular for spelling—the word should be spelled sed)

have (irregular for reading—the *a* should be pronounced as a long vowel; regular for spelling—English base words do not end in *v* so the *e* must be added)

stroke (regular for reading and spelling)

arbor (regular for reading—final *or* in an unaccented syllable is pronounced /er/; irregular for spelling—the most frequent spelling of final /er/ is *er*)

weight (regular for reading—*eigh* is pronounced /ā/; irregular for spelling—the most frequent spelling of medial *a* in a one-syllable word is *a*-consonant-*e*)

soon (regular for reading and spelling)

get (irregular for reading—*g* before *e* should be pronounced /j/; regular for spelling) *bus* (irregular for reading—one final *s* after a short vowel in a one-syllable word is pronounced /z/; irregular for spelling—final *s* after a short vowel in a one-syllable word should be spelled *ss*)

relive (irregular for reading—the *i* should be pronounced as a long vowel; regular for spelling—English words do not end in *v* so the *e* must be added)

ACTIVITY 64—PLANNING LESSONS FOR SPELLING

Answers will vary.

ACTIVITY 65—CONTINUOUS MANUSCRIPT HANDWRITING

1) c, 2) f, 3) l, 4) e, 5) h, 6) k, 7) a, 8) g, 9) j, 10) i, 11) d, 12) b

ACTIVITY 66—APPROACH STROKES FOR CURSIVE LETTERS

Swing up, stop: *i, j, p, r, s, t, u, w*
Push up and over: *m, n, v, x, y, z*
Curve under, over, stop: *a, c, d, g, o, q*
Curve way up, loop left: *b, e, f, h, k, l*

ACTIVITY 67—CURSIVE HANDWRITING STROKE DESCRIPTIONS

1) i, 2) c, 3) d, 4) a, 5) f, 6) h, 7) j, 8) k, 9) g, 10) e, 11) l, 12) b

ACTIVITY 68—HANDWRITING PRACTICE

Introduction and practice activities
1.   Students sky write a new letter while looking at a model. The teacher describes the letter strokes.
2.   Students trace a model of the new letter several times with their fingers.
3.   Students trace a model of a new letter with a pencil.
4.   Students copy a model of a new letter on paper.
5.   Students write a new letter from memory.
Practice activities
6.   Students trace a model of a series of letters that share the same approach stroke.
7.   Students write a dictated series of letters that share the same approach stroke.
8.   Students trace a model of a series of letters that contain different approach strokes.
9.   Students write a dictated series of letters that contain different approach strokes.
10. Students copy words from the board.
11. Students write letters with attention to proportion.

ACTIVITY 69–PLANNING LESSONS FOR HANDWRITING

Answers will vary.

ACTIVITY 70–THE ART AND SCIENCE OF FLUENCY INSTRUCTION

Answers will vary.

ACTIVITY 71–MEASURING PROSODY

Answers will vary.

ACTIVITY 72–TERMS FOR DECODING AND FLUENCY

1) g, 2) o, 3) h, 4) d, 5) a, 6) i, 7) n, 8) l, 9) m, 10) b, 11) f, 12) j, 13) c, 14) e, 15) k, 16) p

ACTIVITY 73–DIALOGUES FOR UNDERSTANDING DIFFICULTIES WITH MATH

Answers will vary.

ACTIVITY 74–MORPHEMES, ORIGINS, MEANINGS, AND DERIVATIVES

The example derivatives do not represent a complete list.

Morpheme	Origin	Meaning	Derivatives
ang	Latin	bend	angle, angular, triangle
astro	Greek	star	astronomy, astrology, astronaut
auto	Greek	self, unaided	autonomy, automatic, autograph
bio	Greek	life	biology, biodegradable, biography
chron	Greek	time	chronicle, chronometer, synchronize
cogn	Latin	know	recognize, cognitive, metacognition
cred	Latin	believe	creed, incredible, credulous
duct	Latin	lead	conduct, induction, deductive
fer	Latin	bear	suffer, infer, refer, confer
geo	Greek	earth	geology, geometry, geodesic
logy	Greek	study of	phonology, morphology, theology
manu	Latin	hand	manual, manuscript, manipulate
pop	Latin	people	population, populace, popular
rupt	Latin	break	interrupt, erupt, irrupt

Morpheme	Origin	Meaning	Derivatives
trans	Latin	across	transport, transfer, transportation
vac	Latin	empty	vacuum, vacate, vacation
vert, vers	Latin	turn	invert, revert, reversible
vis	Latin	see	vision, visible, invisible

ACTIVITY 75–ROOTS AND COMBINING FORMS

(The example derivatives do not represent a complete list.)

ject (to throw): *reject, object, abject, project, eject, subject*

ped (foot): *pedal, pedestal, pedestrian*

spect (to watch): *inspect, respect, spectator, spectacular, speculate*

graph (to write, record): *autograph, photograph, phonograph*

bio (life): *biology, autobiography, biosphere*

ology (study of): *geology, theology, phonology*

syn, syn (same): *synchronize, synagogue, sympathy, symphony*

form (shape): *uniform, formation, transform*

cur (to go, flow): *current, curriculum, concur*

nom (to name): *nominee, nomination, nominal*

greg (to gather, group): *congregate, segregate, integrate, aggregate*

voc (to call): *vocal, vocation, vocabulary, invocation*

nym (to name): *synonym, antonym, pseudonym*

pod (foot): *tripod, podium, podiatrist*

cycl (circle): *bicycle, tricycle, cycle*

struct (to build): *construction, instruction, destruction*

vis (to see): *vision, visible, visor, supervisor*

meter (measure): *thermometer, kilometer, odometer, barometer*

ACTIVITY 76–SYLLABLES AND MORPHEMES

population (4, 2); combination (4, 2); mustang (2, 1); summertime (3, 2); thermostat (3, 2); bumblebee (3, 2); protection (3, 3); wheelbarrow (3, 2); ambulance (3, 2); river (2, 1); watermelon (4, 2); canine (2, 1); dressmaker (3, 3); mercury (3, 1); countryside (3, 2); computing (3, 3); kangaroo (3, 1); vegetables (4, 2)

ACTIVITY 77–CLUES FOR IDENTIFYING WORD ORIGIN

1) The consonant pairs *gn, kn,* and *wr* (Anglo-Saxon); 2) Roots that end in *ct* and *pt* (Latin); 3) Vowel pairs (Anglo-Saxon); 4) Initial consonant clusters *rh, pt, pn,* and *ps* (Greek); 5) Chameleon prefixes (Latin); 6) Common, everyday words (Anglo-Saxon); 7) The consonant cluster *ch* pronounced /k/ (Greek); 8) The letters *c, s,* and *t* pronounced /sh/ (Latin); 9) Medial *y* (Greek); 10) Consonant digraphs *ch, sh, th, wh* (Anglo-Saxon); 11) The affixing of roots (Latin); 12) Compound words (Anglo-Saxon); 13) Combining forms (Greek); 14) The affixing of base words (Anglo-Saxon); 15) The consonant cluster *ph* pronounced /f/ (Greek); 16) The schwa or unstressed vowel sound (Latin)

ACTIVITY 78–IDENTIFYING WORD ORIGIN

scholar (Greek), dislike (Anglo-Saxon), that (Anglo-Saxon), construction (Latin), phonograph (Greek), made (Anglo-Saxon), excellent (Latin), boat (Anglo-Saxon), conductor (Latin), barn (Anglo-Saxon), microscope (Greek), direction (Latin), transport (Latin), symphony (Greek), chloroplast (Greek), hardware (Anglo-Saxon), photograph (Greek), shipyard (Anglo-Saxon), respect (Latin), spatial (Latin), water (Anglo-Saxon), manuscript (Latin), timely (Anglo-Saxon), portable (Latin), heart (Anglo-Saxon), good (Anglo-Saxon), introduction (Latin), transcript (Latin), bread (Anglo-Saxon), bad (Anglo-Saxon)

ACTIVITY 79–IDENTIFYING WORD ORIGINS

food (Anglo-Saxon), rhythm (Greek), lotion (Latin), reject (Latin), eruption (Latin), chorus (Greek), thermometer (Greek), gather (Anglo-Saxon), induction (Latin), intersect (Latin), psychology (Greek), rhododendron (Greek), helpless (Anglo-Saxon), napkin (Anglo-Saxon), wait (Anglo-Saxon), destruction (Latin), sympathy (Greek), football (Anglo-Saxon), illegal (Latin), conduct (Latin)

ACTIVITY 80–SYLLABLES AND MORPHEMES

instructor (3, 3); autograph (3, 2); destruction (3, 3); salamander (4, 1); unleaded (3,3); waits (1, 2); interjection; (4, 3); bookkeeper (3, 3); conjunction (3, 3); photographic (4, 3); rattlesnake (3, 2); marker (2, 2); cucumber (3, 1); barbecue (3, 1); manuscript (3, 2); outstanding (3, 3); handshake (2, 2); bluebonnet (3, 2)

ACTIVITY 81–SEMANTIC WORD WEBS

Answers will vary.

ACTIVITY 82–DERIVATIVE WORD WEBS

Answers will vary.

ACTIVITY 83–MULTIPLE MEANING WEBS

Answers will vary.

ACTIVITY 84–WORD PROFILES

Word: like

Number of phonemes: 3   Phonemes: /l/, /ī/, /k/

Rime pattern: *ike* as in *bike, hike, Mike, pike, strike*

Number of letters: 4   Letters: l, i, k, e

Number of graphemes: 3   Graphemes: l, i-e, k

Spelling pattern(s): medial /ī/ in a one-syllable base word is spelled *i*-consonant-e; or final /k/ after a long vowel is spelled *ke*.

Origin: Anglo-Saxon

Derivatives: likeness, liked, likes, homelike

Answers to other parts of the word profile will vary.

ACTIVITY 85–WORD PROFILES

Answers may vary.

Word: play

Number of phonemes: 3   Phonemes: /p/, /l/, /ā/

Rime pattern: *ay* as in *bay, day, hay, lay, may, pay, ray, say, stay, tray, slay*

Number of letters: 4   Letters: p, l, a, y

Number of graphemes: 3   Graphemes: p, l, ay

Spelling pattern(s): final /ā/ is spelled *ay*

Origin: Anglo-Saxon

Derivatives: playful, player, plays, played

Answers to other parts of the word profile will vary.

ACTIVITY 86–SEMANTIC FEATURE ANALYSIS

Answers will vary.

ACTIVITY 87–TIERS OF VOCABULARY WORDS

Tier One	Tier Two*	Tier Three*
hunt napkin health forest knowledge happening	relate important erupt declare interpret discontent featured specific	esophagus rhetoric dysplasia euphemism geriatric protoplasm

*Tier Two and Three words may vary according to students' experiences.

ACTIVITY 88–STUDENT-FRIENDLY DEFINITIONS

Answers will vary.

ACTIVITY 89–PRECISION IN USE OF VOCABULARY

Answers will vary, but the less intensive words might include *down, low, sad, glum, blue, sullen, cheerless, forlorn, gloomy, disappointed, sorrowful, somber,* and *discontented.*

The more intensive words might include *despondent, disconsolate, devastated, pessimistic, depressed, distraught,* and *dejected.*

Because of the rain, the picnic was canceled, and the children were (*sad, disappointed, glum,* etc.) but not (*distraught, depressed, despondent,* and so forth).

The hurricane completely destroyed the town, and the people were not just (*gloomy, forlorn, cheerless,* etc.); they were (*devastated, distraught, despondent,* and so forth).

Example of gradient antonyms for *unhappy: satisfied, content, pleased, glad, happy, delighted, cheerful, joyful, merry, bubbly, thrilled, excited, jovial, buoyant, overjoyed, elated, ecstatic, exhilarated, euphoric, rapturous*

ACTIVITY 90–COMPREHENSION: SUMMARIZATION

Answers will vary.

ACTIVITY 91–COMPREHENSION: TEXT-DEPENDENT QUESTIONS AND SUMMARIZATION

Answers will vary.

   Possible text-dependent questions: What might the moral of this story be and what evidence supports your answer? What evidence in text suggests the setting of the story? Based on the text, how does Georgiana attend to her task? Based on the text, what might the word *scoffed* mean?

ACTIVITY 92–PARTS OF SPEECH

1. Three homes at Fifth Street and Pine burned. (adj., noun, prep., noun, noun, conj., noun, verb)

2. That dog ran home. (adj., noun, verb, adv.)

3. The red shirts will run in hot water. (adj., adj., noun, verb, verb, prep., adj., noun)

4. Well, I have another run in my sock. (interj., pron., verb, adj., noun, prep., adj., noun)

5. The play last night was fun. (adj., noun, adj., noun, verb, adj.)

6. He left his book on the bus yesterday. (pron., verb, adj., noun, prep., adj., noun, adv.)

7. Those students have no time for fun and games. (adj., noun, verb, adv., noun, prep., noun, conj., noun)

8. No, the teacher said we must finish our assignment. (interj., adj., noun, verb, pron., verb, verb, adj., noun)

9. Many children happily played a game. (adj., noun, adv., verb, adj., noun)

10. Two big events are planned for this year. (adj., adj., noun, verb, verb, prep., adj., noun)

ACTIVITY 93–SYNTAX

Answers will vary.

ACTIVITY 94–COMPOSITION: THE DESCRIPTIVE PARAGRAPH

Answers will vary.

ACTIVITY 95–COMPOSITION: WRITING A DESCRIPTIVE PARAGRAPH

Answers will vary.

ACTIVITY 96–COMPOSITION: WRITING AN ARGUMENT PARAGRAPH

Answers will vary.

ACTIVITY 97–COMPOSITION: THE EFFORTLESS PARAGRAPH

Answers will vary.

ACTIVITY 98–COMPOSITION: TRANSITION WORDS AND PHRASES

Time and sequence: *first, finally, before*

Emphasis: *obviously, above all, keep in mind*
Change of direction: *yet, otherwise, certainly*
Illustration: *for example, specifically, as an illustration*
Conclusion: *therefore, thus, in summary*

ACTIVITY 99–PLANNING LESSONS FOR PHONOLOGICAL AWARENESS, ALPHABET KNOWLEDGE, AND HISTORY OF LANGUAGE

Answers will vary.

ACTIVITY 100–PLANNING LESSONS FOR BEGINNING READING

Answers will vary.

ACTIVITY 101–SPANISH PHONEMES

English consonant sound **with cognate in Spanish:** /m/ (yes), /s/ (yes), /sh/ (no), /t/ (yes), /d/ (yes), /j/ (no), /zh/ (no), /k/ (yes), /th/ (no) (*Note:* The unvoiced /th/ sound and the /zh/ sound are used in Castilian Spanish.)

Spanish consonant sound **with cognate in English:** /rr/ (no), /b/ (yes), /ñ/ (no), /p/ (yes), /g/ (yes), /f/ (yes), /ch/ (yes), /l/ (yes)

ACTIVITY 102–REASON FOR FINAL *e*

Word	Reason for Silent *e*	Derivatives
name	Vowel-consonant-*e*	naming, named, nameless
shave	Vowel-consonant-*e*; base words do not end in *v*	shaving, shaved, shaver
battle	Consonant-*le*	battling, battled, battlement
infringe	Soft *g*	infringing, infringer, infringement
trace	Vowel-consonant-*e* and soft *c*	tracing, traced, traceable

ACTIVITY 103–CREATING AN EDUCATIONAL MEMORIES SAMPLE

Answers will vary.

Educational Memories samples will vary. See Chapter 21 in Birsh and Carreker (2018) for sample excerpts and further discussion of Educational Memories.

ACTIVITIES COORDINATED WITH
BECOMING A PROFESSIONAL READING TEACHER
(AARON, JOSHI, & QUATROCHE, 2008)

Chapter 3–The Psycholinguistics of Spoken Language

Activities 7, 8, 9, 10, 11, 12, 13, 14, 15, 17, 18, 19, 20

Chapter 4–The Psycholinguistics of Written Language

Activities 4, 5, 6, 21, 22, 40, 41

Chapter 5–Development of Spoken and Written Language Skills

Activities 28, 29, 30, 31

Chapter 6–Developing Basic Literacy Skills

Activities 16, 23, 24, 25, 26

Chapter 7–Strategies for Developing Decoding, Instant Word Reading, and Spelling Skills

Activities 16, 33, 34, 35, 36, 37, 38, 39, 42, 43, 44, 45, 46, 47, 48, 49, 50, 51, 52, 53, 54, 55, 56, 57, 58, 59, 60, 61, 62, 63, 64, 65, 66, 67, 68, 69, 70, 71, 72, 73, 74, 75, 99

Chapter 8–Strategies for Developing Vocabulary Knowledge, Comprehension Skills, and Writing Skills

Activities 76, 77, 78, 79, 80, 81, 82, 83, 84, 85, 86, 87, 88, 89, 90, 91, 92, 93, 94, 95, 96, 97, 98

References

Aaron, P.G., Joshi, R.M., & Quatroche, D. (2008). *Becoming a professional reading teacher*. Baltimore, MD: Paul H. Brookes Publishing Co.

Adams, M.J. (1990). *Beginning to read: Thinking and learning about print*. Cambridge, MA: The MIT Press.

Barrutia, R., & Schwegler, A. (1994). *Fonética y fonología espanõlas* [Spanish phonics and phonology] (2nd ed.). New York, NY: John Wiley & Sons.

Beck, I.L., McKeown, M.G., & Kucan, L. (2013). *Bringing words to life: Robust vocabulary instruction* (2nd ed.). New York, NY: Guilford Press.

Birsh, J.R., & Carreker, S. (Eds.). (2018). *Multisensory teaching of basic language skills* (4th ed.). Baltimore, MD: Paul H. Brookes Publishing Co.

Birsh, J.R., Schedler, J.F., & Singer, R. (2018). Planning multisensory structured language lessons and the classroom environment. In J.R. Birsh & S. Carreker (Eds.), *Multisensory teaching of basic language skills* (4th ed., pp. 679-717). Baltimore, MD: Paul H. Brookes Publishing Co.

Blumenthal, S.H (2018). Working with high functioning adults with dyslexia and other academic challenges. In J.R. Birsh & S. Carreker (Eds.), *Multisensory teaching of basic language skills* (4th ed., pp. 794-814). Baltimore, MD: Paul H. Brookes Publishing Co.

Cárdenas-Hagan, E. (2018). Language and literacy development among English language learners. In J.R. Birsh & S. Carreker (Eds.), *Multisensory teaching of basic language skills* (4th ed., pp. 719-756). Baltimore, MD: Paul H. Brookes Publishing Co.

Carreker, S. (1992). *Scientific spelling*. Bellaire, TX: Neuhaus Education Center.

Carreker, S. (2002). *Scientific spelling*. Bellaire, TX: Neuhaus Education Center.

Carreker, S. (2004). *Developing metacognitive skills*. Bellaire, TX: Neuhaus Education Center.

Carreker, S. (2018a). Teaching reading: Accurate decoding. In J.R. Birsh & S. Carreker (Eds.), *Multisensory teaching of basic language skills* (4th ed., pp. 338-388). Baltimore, MD: Paul H. Brookes Publishing Co.

Carreker, S. (2018b). Teaching spelling. In J.R. Birsh & S. Carreker (Eds.), *Multisensory teaching of basic language skills* (4th ed., pp. 389-434). Baltimore, MD: Paul H. Brookes Publishing Co.

Cox, A.R. (1992). *Foundations for literacy: Structures and techniques for multisensory teaching of basic written English skills*. Cambridge, MA: Educators Publishing Service.

Farrell, M.L., & Cushen-White, N. (2018). Multisensory structured language education. In J.R. Birsh & S. Carreker (Eds.), *Multisensory teaching of basic language skills* (4th ed., pp. 35-80). Baltimore, MD: Paul H. Brookes Publishing Co.

Foorman, B.R., & Schatschneider, C. (1997). Beyond alphabetic reading: Comments on Torgesen's prevention and intervention studies. *Journal of Academic Language Therapy, 1*, 59-65.

Geary, D.C. (2004). Mathematics and learning disabilities. *Journal of Learning Disabilities, 37*(1), 4-15. doi:10.1177/00222194040370010201

Good, R.H., & Kiminski, R.A. (2002). *Dynamic Indicators of Basic Early Literacy Skills (DIBELS)*. Eugene, OR: Institute for the Development of Education Achievement.

Hennessy, N.E. (2018). Working with word meaning: Vocabulary instruction. In J.R. Birsh & S. Carreker (Eds.), *Multisensory teaching of basic language skills* (4th ed., pp. 558-599). Baltimore, MD: Paul H. Brookes Publishing Co.

Henry, M.K. (1988). Beyond phonics: Integrating decoding and spelling instruction based on word origin and structure. *Annals of Dyslexia, 38*, 259-277.

Henry, M.K. (2010). *Unlocking literacy: Effective decoding and spelling instruction* (2nd ed.). Baltimore, MD: Paul H. Brookes Publishing Co.

Henry, M.K. (2018). The history and structure of written English. In J.R. Birsh & S. Carreker (Eds.), *Multisensory teaching of basic language skills* (4th ed., pp. 539-557). Baltimore, MD: Paul H. Brookes Publishing Co.

Invernizzi, M., Meier, J., & Juel, C. (2002). *Phonological Awareness Screening 1-3 (PALS)*. Charlottesville: University of Virginia.

Kaufman, C. (2011). *Executive function in the classroom: Practical strategies for improving performance and enhancing skills for all students*. Baltimore, MD: Paul H. Brookes Publishing Co.

Kosc, L. (1974). Developmental dyscalculia. *Journal of Learning Disabilities, 7,* 164-77.

Marzola, E.S. (2018). Strategies to improve reading comprehension in the multisensory classroom. In J.R. Birsh & S. Carreker (Eds.), *Multisensory teaching of basic language skills* (4th ed., pp. 600-645). Baltimore, MD: Paul H. Brookes Publishing Co.

Merriam Webster's collegiate dictionary (11th ed.). (2011). Springfield, MA: Merriam-Webster.

Moats, L.C. (1995). *Spelling: Development, disabilities and instruction*. Timonium, MD: York Press.

Moats, L.C. (2010). *Speech to print: Language essentials for teachers*. Baltimore, MD: Paul H. Brookes Publishing Co.

Paulson, L.H. (2018). Teaching phonemic awareness. In J.R. Birsh & S. Carreker (Eds.), *Multisensory teaching of basic language skills* (4th ed., pp. 205-256). Baltimore, MD: Paul H. Brookes Publishing Co.

Read, C. (1971). Pre-school children's knowledge of English phonology. *Harvard Educational Review, 41,* 1-34.

Rourke, B., & Conway, J.A. (1997). Disabilities of arithmetic and mathematical reasoning: Perspectives from neurology and neuropsychology. *Journal of Learning Disabilities, 30*(1), 34-46.

Rumsey, J.M. (1996). Neuroimaging in developmental dyslexia: A review and conceptualization. In G.R. Lyon & J.M. Rumsey (Eds.), *Neuroimaging: A window to the neurological foundation of learning and behavior in children* (pp. 57-77). Baltimore, MD: Paul H. Brookes Publishing Co.

Soifer, L.H. (2018). Oral language development and its relationship to literacy. In J.R. Birsh & S. Carreker (Eds.), *Multisensory teaching of basic language skills* (4th ed., pp. 81-139). Baltimore, MD: Paul H. Brookes Publishing Co.

Stanback, M.L. (1992). Analysis of frequency-based vocabulary of 17,602 words. *Annals of Dyslexia, 42,* 196-221.

Steere, A., Peck, C.Z., & Kahn, L. (1984). *Solving language difficulties: Remedial routines*. Cambridge, MA: Educators Publishing Service.

Stock, P., Desoete, A., & Roeyers, H. (2006). Focusing on mathematical disabilities: A search for definition, classification and assessment. In S.V. Randall (Ed.), *Learning disabilities: New research* (pp. 29-62). Hauppage, NY: Nova Science.

Texas Scottish Rite Hospital for Children, Child Development Division. (1996). *Teaching cursive writing* [Brochure]. Dallas, TX; Author.

von Aster, M. (2000). Developmental cognitive neuropsychology of number processing and calculation: Varieties of developmental dyscalculia. *European Child & Adolescent Psychiatry, 9*(Suppl 2), S41. doi:10.1007/s007870070008

Wilson, B.A. (2018). Instruction for older students with a word-level reading disability. In J.R. Birsh & S. Carreker (Eds.), *Multisensory teaching of basic language skills* (4th ed., pp. 757-793). Baltimore, MD: Paul H. Brookes Publishing Co.

Wolf, B.J., & Berninger, V. (2018). Teaching handwriting. In J.R. Birsh & S. Carreker (Eds.), *Multisensory teaching of basic language skills* (4th ed., pp. 435-466). Baltimore, MD: Paul H. Brookes Publishing Co.